W9-BGS-488

Nothing Will Separate Us

A widow's
memoir
of faith, grace
and
miracles
since 9/11

DONNA KILLOUGHEY BIRD
As told to Charlotte Rogers Brown

Geraldine ~
from one
teller of
stories to
another...

...We are all
connected

TEMPE, AZ
10-31-15

dkilloughey@gmail.com

Nothing Will Separate Us
A widow's memoir of faith, grace & miracles since 9/11

© 2011 by Donna Killoughey Bird
As told to Charlotte Rogers Brown

Excerpts from *To Kill a Mockingbird*, © 1960 by Harper Lee reprinted by permission of HarperCollins Publishers.

Excerpts from *Cowboy*, © 2010 by Rocco Wachman and Matt Pellegrini reprinted by permission of HarperCollins Publishers.

ALL RIGHTS RESERVED. No part of this book may be reproduced, stored in a retrieval system, or transmitted by any means, electronic, mechanical, photocopying, recording or otherwise without written permission from the author.

ISBN 978-0-615-51159-7
Library of Congress Control Number: 2011912093

Graphic design by Squadron Design

Published by Bird Seeds Publishing, LLC Tempe, AZ

To Gary

While many of us were touched in some personal way by the tragic events of 9/11, most Americans did not lose loved ones and have little insight into the personal stories of the victims and their families. In *Nothing Will Separate Us*, Donna Killoughey Bird shares the personal story of her husband, their family, their love, faith and devotion. I knew Gary professionally and have had the pleasure of getting to know Donna in the years since we named a risk management award in his honor. Her book made me smile and cry and smile again as I came to know and respect Gary for the gentleman cowboy he was while being reminded of the power of faith above all else.

Jack P. Gibson, President & CEO International Risk Management Institute, Inc.

This is a wonderful story, at once funny, poignant and spiritual. It is a sweet remembrance of a too-short life. Despite the tragedy of 9/11, there is joy in every chapter of this book.

Donna J. Marino, President and CEO, Catholic Community Foundation, Phoenix

Donna Killoughey Bird offers a tender remembrance of her beloved husband, Gary Bird, and chronicles her family's journey after his death in New York City on September 11, 2001. Under a national spotlight, buoyed by her religious faith, she nurtured her family through seemingly unbearable grief to acceptance and peace.

Monica Bay, Editor-in-Chief, Law Technology News, New York City

Donna Killoughey Bird beautifully articulates the deep loss that she experienced on that fateful September 11. But this book is so much more than a story of loss: it is a story of love, of hope, of acceptance. It is the story of how one courageous person has chosen to live her life in the wake of what many would otherwise see as hopeless. Her life is a Journey that will profoundly touch all lives, regardless of whether we have personally experienced such a loss, or if ours is yet to come.

Steve Zabilski, Executive Director, Society of St. Vincent de Paul, Phoenix

Nothing Will Separate Us is a narrative of faith, acceptance, forgiveness, healing and spiritual growth. This book is a source of comfort and inspiration to those dealing with the pain of sudden and unexpected loss.

Msgr. Richard Moyer, Phoenix, AZ

Contents

Foreword

I met Donna Killoughey Bird at a café in Tempe in February 2010. Until then I had never met anyone who lost a loved one in the tragic events of 9/11. Over the next fifteen months as she and I worked together on the writing of this book, I did my best to place myself in her shoes—in the shoes of a woman who lost a husband she loved and expected to grow old with.

My husband Charlie and I celebrated our seventeenth wedding anniversary this past April. On May 21 Donna and I spent the day together gathering photos and documents for the book's graphic designer to scan into his computer. At some point that afternoon, Donna turned to me and said she wanted to read aloud the passage in the book that outlines what she knows to be true about our eternal connection to God and each other. I thought it a little odd that she wanted to read the passage aloud to me, particularly since I already knew what it said. All the same I found myself closing my eyes and listening intently to every word.

Later that evening, shortly after I returned home, my beloved Charlie lay down to take a nap and passed away in his sleep. Throughout the months I worked with Donna on this book, I found myself praying these words: "Please, God, don't let this be preparing me for something."

I can't imagine where I would be right now, what I would be feeling and experiencing, had I not met Donna and become so intimately involved in telling her story. I can't imagine anything that could have prepared me more to bear the loss of my husband, my best friend, my Charlie. I've never seen greater evidence of God's plan and God's love than the knowledge that, not only was I the first to hear the full story of Donna's journey of faith in the midst of loss, I am the first to draw strength and courage from it. As I write this, my grief is still new. Charlie passed a month ago today. Every night I awaken from sleep and for a second or two, my world is the same as it was. Then I remember: Charlie is gone. I relive the terrible shock of his passing every night, several times a night, until morning comes and I get on with the painful business of learning how to live without him.

In many ways Charlie and Donna's husband, Gary, were very different men, although they were both born in 1950, just three months apart. After high school, Charlie attended Chico State University where he grew his hair down to his waist, spent his summers sitting cross-legged in a teepee practicing Transcendental Meditation and prepared for his future as a social liberal working exclusively for non-profits. Meanwhile Gary was at the University of Arizona developing his conservative philosophies and preparing for a corporate career—between summers spent on horseback, dressed in his Wrangler jeans and cowboy hat.

Yet in the ways that matter most, Charlie and Gary were very much alike. Both loved and advocated for children—Gary through his commitment to the Tempe Boys and Girls Club and Charlie through his long career with Head Start.

Both men put family first and loved unconditionally. Both revered nature. Both practiced their spirituality in their own ways and respected the need for others to do the same.

Both are deeply missed by everyone who loved them.

That first day Donna and I sat together at the café, she told me she wanted to write a book to help others find peace in the midst of loss, any kind of loss. A loved one. A cherished home. A healthy body. Financial security.

This is that book. My sincere desire is that, whatever your loss may be, you are able to draw strength, comfort and peace from these pages. Just as I do now.

We are never alone.

– Charlotte Rogers Brown

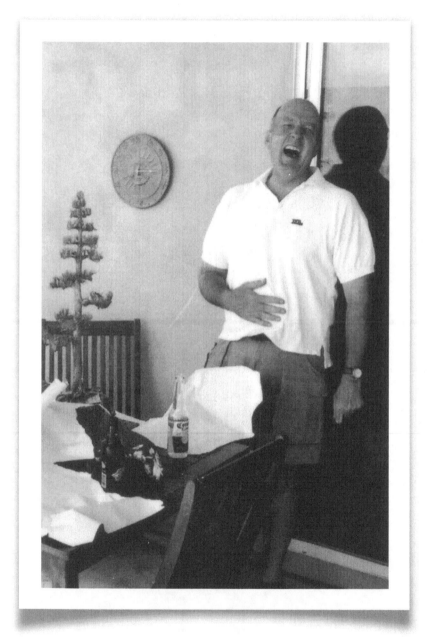

Gary Bird
(July 2001)

Nothing Will Separate Us

Preface

On September 24, 2001, my cousin Gloria sat at her computer in Southern California to make airline reservations for her and her family's upcoming trip to Arizona. She typed in all the pertinent information:

Last name: Krainock

Number of passengers: 4

Departure date: October 3, 2001

Departing from: San Diego

Arriving in: Phoenix

With the itinerary set and billing completed, Gloria waited for her receipt with the confirmation code—the random series of letters—she would need to present at the airport in exchange for boarding passes. Of the hundreds of millions of possible six-letter combinations, this is what came up on her computer screen:

TRBIRD

T...R...BIRD

Gloria stared at her computer screen, stunned by what she saw. It wasn't just that the letters spelled a word in the English language, although she found that unusual enough. As a former reservation agent/customer service representative for America West Airlines, she had seen thousands of confirmation codes but not one that contained an actual word.

It was the word itself that made Gloria catch her breath. The reservations were for Gloria and her family to fly to Phoenix to attend the memorial service for my husband—the only resident of Arizona killed in the World Trade Center on 9/11.

His name was Gary ***Bird.***

Krainock, Gloria
From: PNR-america west airlines [web.master@americawest.com]
Sent: Monday, September 24, 2001 10:28 PM
Subject: KRAINOCK, BRUCE

Thank you for booking your reservation on americawest.com. Below is your confirmation. If you require assistance with your reservation, please contact America West Reservations at 800-235-9292.

An OFFICIAL receipt for business purposes may be obtained at any America West ticket counter or gate PRIOR to completion of travel.

RECEIPT

Your E-Ticket was issued
As with all airline tickets it is not transferable.
This is a receipt only and has no cash value.
Seats selected online are requests only, are based on availability and subject to change.

Confirmation Number:TRBIRD

Issued: Mon Sep 24 22:27:40 2001

Name(s) of people traveling:

Passenger #1: Bruce Krainock
Ticket Number: 2716071446
Passenger #2: Gloria Krainock
Ticket Number: 2716071447
Passenger #3: Brian Krainock
Ticket Number: 2716071448
Passenger #4: Kevin Krainock
Ticket Number: 2716071449

ITINERARY

Flight: America West Airline 199

A/C: Boeing 737-300
Depart: SAN/San Diego, CA/Wednesday October 3 7:35 pm
Arrive: PHX/Phoenix, AZ/Wednesday October 3 8:49 pm
Stops: non-stop Miles:304
Seats Requested: 9C 9D 9B 9E
Cabin: Coach

Introduction

My husband Gary often took Metro Bus #241 from Tempe to his office in downtown Phoenix, not because he was a practical person—although he was—but because he enjoyed spending time with people. He enjoyed talking with them, working with them, playing with them, learning from them and, most of all, helping them live the best lives possible.

One day a letter came from a woman whom I never met, but who frequently encountered Gary on that morning commute. She wrote:

> *I remember chatting with Gary on several occasions while waiting for the bus. We talked about his trip to Chile as well as current events. It was obvious to my other bus mates and me that he was an intelligent man who thought through issues and had real common sense. He was a likable man who always had a kind word for whomever he spoke with.*
>
> *But his true colors really came through on those days when the bus was full. When a woman got on the bus to find all seats taken, Gary was the first person to give up his seat.*
>
> *Every time.*
>
> *I believe it was second nature to him. That is the kind of person he was.*

Gary was known in many circles for a great many things. In our city of Tempe, Arizona, he was known for his community service and leadership with, among others, the Tempe Boys and Girls Club, the Planning and Zoning Commission and the Tempe Jaycees.

To his colleagues in the field of risk management, he was known as much for the trail rides he guided across his native Arizona desert lands as he was for his authoritative text on the installation and operation of owner-controlled insurance programs.

Those with more personal connections with Gary—his parents, grandparents, sisters, brother and friends—knew him as an animal lover, sports enthusiast, cowboy, gentleman, selfless giver and champion of children.

Our children, Amanda and Andrew, knew him as a loving and devoted dad who sang them to sleep when they were babies, taught them to ski and ride horses, and never let them forget how valuable they are.

I knew and treasured Gary as my wonderful companion from the first moment we met.

Even people who enjoyed only the briefest encounters with Gary—his fellow commuters, for instance—recognized him as a man who took an interest in other people, who would gladly put their comfort ahead of his own.

Every time.

Yet type the words *Gary Bird Tempe Arizona* into any search engine and what comes up will suggest that what is most significant about him is not how he lived but how he died. That what sets him apart is the fact he was the only person from the Grand Canyon State to die in the World Trade Center on September 11. It was his second, and final, day of orientation meetings for his new job at Marsh USA. He likely had his suitcase with him—packed with his carefully chosen clothes and favorite CDs—because he was getting on a plane in just a few hours.

"I'll be home for dinner Tuesday night." Those were among his last words to me as he left our home early Sunday morning. Those and "I love you."

This book is not about what set Gary apart from other people, but about what I have learned—while he was alive and after his death—about what makes us all inseparable. This book is not about the tragedy of Gary's sudden passing, but about the miracles of faith, family, friendship and community that endured.

People of all faiths were killed in the terrorist attacks, just as people of all faiths reached out and were a source of strength to my family and me as we mourned our loss. Although I am a "cradle Catholic"—baptized and raised in the Catholic Church—I am not a theologian or scholar of church doctrine. I include elements of Catholicism on these pages only because it is the religion my children and I practice. It serves as the backdrop of our faith and as such, plays an integral role in our story. I have no desire to make a case for any particular religion or spiritual practice. Perhaps nothing speaks to that better than the fact that, while he went to church with us almost every Sunday, Gary chose not to officially "convert." He felt no need to. He believed that worshiping God required no particular affiliation, only that he live the best life he could.

At Gary's memorial celebration, the pastor of our church joked, "You know times have changed when a Catholic priest stands at the pulpit and tells you, for sure, that a non-Catholic is in heaven."

In the days immediately following the terrorist attacks—before we knew whether Gary had survived—my doctor wrote me two prescriptions. The first was for something to help me sleep. On another sheet he wrote, *Romans 8:28 to end of chapter.*

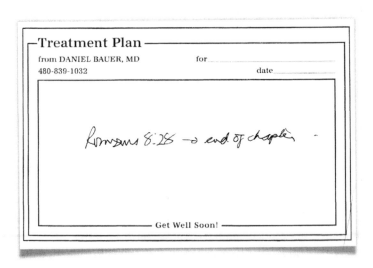

When I got home, I took out my Bible and read the passage he prescribed:

> *...For I am convinced that neither death nor life, neither angels nor demons, neither the present nor the future, nor any powers, neither height nor depth, nor anything else in all creation, will be able to separate us from the love of God that is in Christ Jesus our Lord.*

Throughout the minutes, hours, days, months and years since American Airlines Flight 11 crashed into the World Trade Center's North Tower—where the Marsh USA offices between the ninety-third and ninety-ninth floors constituted the entire impact zone—I've come to believe those words with a depth and certainty that will never leave me. Nothing, *nothing* that happened on that September morning could ever separate me from the love of God. I would soon come to know that nothing—not death, not the work of terrorists—could separate me from the love of my husband, children, family, friends, community and compassionate strangers who reached out to me from around the globe.

I came to know this because there were signs that pointed to the peace of God that surpasses all understanding. Signs that comforted me, strengthened me and guided me. The signs came in many forms—some as simple and yet as mystifying as Gary's name showing up on a random confirmation code, and others that can only be described as mystical. God provided countless instruments of peace. Among them was that woman Gary met on Metro Bus 241.

I admired him and even though I did not know him well (we did not know each other's names), I had tremendous respect for him. I am certain that when the plane crashed into the building, he would have done everything he could to help those around him before trying to help himself. I am sure of it, because he showed me he was that kind of person when we rode the bus together in Tempe.

For anyone facing a dark time, I hope these pages bring strength and comfort. I hope that through our family's story, you will come to know and trust that you, too, are never alone or separate.

I want you to come to know Gary as we knew him. Our family photo albums show us for who we are—amateurs who don't always have the camera in focus and who are prone to cutting off feet or the tops of heads. Our letters to family and friends wouldn't win any literary prizes and our family videos sometimes stop short at critical moments for failure to bring enough batteries. Yet as imperfect as they are, the souvenirs we've treasured over the years tell the story of a man who gave us so many reasons to never want to say "goodbye." Among these pages I've included many of our keepsakes—including some of the hundreds of messages we've received from people around the world—so you can see not what we lost, but all the richness Gary left with us.

Only then can you see the miracles in the rest of our story.

Family Album

You are looking at a scene from our wedding reception in 1982. In the foreground is a small, blurred image of the top of our six-tiered wedding cake, a confectionery masterpiece constructed with white pillars and stairways lined with miniature attendants over a bubbling fountain.

Missing from the photograph are the basketball hoops, electronic scoreboard and drinking fountains mounted on the wall. We held our reception in the gymnasium at the Tempe Boys and Girls Club. We did so for two reasons. Both practical people, Gary and I agreed that since we wanted a wedding and a honeymoon in Tahiti, the bulk of our money would best be spent on the honeymoon. My mother sewed my wedding gown, my cousin loaned me the veil she wore in her wedding and we got the use of the gymnasium for free.

Aside from the attractiveness of the rental fee, the other, even more compelling reason we chose that site was because of the special meaning it held for Gary. As a founding member of the Tempe Boys and Girls Club, Gary had helped raise the capital that built the gymnasium. For him it was a place to "see the beaming faces and hear the laughter of the children"—the words he would later write for an article about the project.

We could not have chosen a more fitting, more joyous place to celebrate our new life together than in a place celebrated by children and families.

Home Movies

In preparing to write this book, I took all of our home movies taped in VHS format to a place that transfers them onto DVDs. On free evenings I'd curl up on the couch with some flat bread, brie and a glass of red wine and watch reruns of my life with Gary and our children. Like many couples, we bought our first video camera just before the birth of our first child. Neither of us had operated a video camera previously, a fact that is painfully obvious when I came across our recording of Amanda's baptism. Almost the entire film looks as though it was filmed below deck on the Andrea Gale during the perfect storm. At times the lens appears to zoom in and out of its own accord. At others it swings wildly upward, stopping briefly on the image of a ceiling light before swooping downward to the floor past various men's and women's shoes. Anyone who dares watch it should consider taking Dramamine first.

Now and then either my voice or Gary's can be heard saying things like, "Is the light still on?" or "Push the red button again."

In our defense, Gary and I weren't the only ones operating the camera that morning. Sometimes we passed it off to a friend so that Gary, Amanda and I could all be in the shot with Amanda's godparents. Unfortunately, many people in the early 1980s were unrehearsed at camera handling.

Yet amid all the blurred images, one clear, precious one comes into view: Amanda supported in Gary's arms as the priest pours the holy water on the top of her tiny head.

Breaking News

Katie Couric was the first to let me know that something unthinkable might have happened to my husband.

"We have breaking news," I heard her say as I was getting ready for work. When I looked at the television to see what it was, I saw smoke pouring from one of the towers at the World Trade Center where Gary was scheduled for a morning meeting at the offices of Marsh USA, a company specializing in risk management and insurance. I grabbed the phone and dialed Mike Goss, the director of Marsh's Phoenix office and a close friend of Gary's. Mike was still in bed when I called. I asked him to turn on his television and tell me whether the Marsh offices were in the burning building that appeared on the screen.

I don't know how much time passed before I heard Mike's voice again, telling me not to worry, that the fire was in the North Tower and that Marsh was located in the other, undamaged tower.

Relieved to know that Gary most likely was safe, I began sharing the events of the past few days with Mike, who knew nothing of Gary's last-minute trip to New York. Gary had planned to be in Denver on September 11, giving a presentation at a national risk management conference, but that was before Marsh offered him what he considered his "dream job" as Senior Vice President working with a new international construction risk management team. When his new employer asked if he could come to New York City for one day of orientation followed by a brief meeting with the new team, Gary quickly set about rearranging his plans. That was Friday, September 7.

Before he left on Sunday morning, Gary mentioned to me that he would be going to the World Trade Center for a meeting in one of the Marsh offices.

"The building is so high, you have to change elevators on the fifty-second floor," he said and we laughed.

Then, as he always did before leaving to go anywhere in the morning, he stopped by the kids' rooms to say "goodbye."

Amanda was just stepping out of the shower, so she and her father simply called out their goodbyes through the bathroom door. A few moments later, Amanda felt the impulse to throw on her bathrobe and run after him. She stepped out of the bathroom and looked around, disappointed to find the hallway and dining room empty.

Just then Gary appeared from around a corner and stopped to look out the window. Amanda ran over and threw her arms around him, hugging him for what she would later say felt like a full ten minutes.

Then Gary went to his truck and drove away, while the children and I went on with our own Sunday plans.

Gary and I frequently neglected to leave behind a copy of our itineraries when we traveled on business. We both trusted each other to take care of things at home and to check in by telephone when our work schedules allowed. This trip to New York was to be such a short one that when Gary left, I never gave a thought to the fact that I didn't even know where he was staying.

I had a full schedule myself that Monday, so that between work and the children, it was well into the evening before I had a moment to consider calling Gary to ask how he felt about his first day at his new job. I was about to dial his cell phone number when I remembered the three-hour time difference between Tempe and New York. I decided not to risk waking him—especially considering I would hear all the details the next evening at dinner.

And now Katie Couric was on television telling me my husband might be in terrible trouble. I was still on the phone with Mike when the plane hit the second tower. Mike remembers me screaming, but I honestly have no memory of that moment.

What I do remember is that after I got off the phone with Mike, I went to Amanda's and Andrew's bedrooms. I told them their Dad might be near a building that was struck by an airplane in New York and that we all needed to pray. Together we decided the best thing to do was for me to take them on to school. We stopped on the way to pick up a neighbor boy and together we all heard the description on the radio of the South Tower collapsing. I remember hoping that, since the South Tower was the second tower hit, Gary had enough time to get out of the building, or at least make it to a level where he could be rescued. I hoped my cell phone would ring and I would hear Gary's voice on the other end telling me he got my messages and that, yes, he was safe.

In those first few, uncertain hours of September 11, I knew exactly what I was supposed to do. For as though one might think it impossible for such opposing feelings to occupy the same space within a single mind, a single heart and a single soul, amid the fear and anguish I felt from the moment I saw the smoke pouring out of the World Trade Center, the feeling I felt most powerfully and continuously was...peace.

After dropping off the children at their respective schools, I drove straight to my church. It was the only place I knew to seek comfort.

Family Album

I was raised in the Catholic Church by two church-going parents. Gary's family called themselves "Protestants" but were much more likely to spend their Sunday mornings on horseback than in a pew. So when Gary and I were planning for our marriage, he had no strong feelings one way or the other about where to worship as a couple and future parents. My faith required that we go through marriage preparedness classes prior to the wedding and Gary participated willingly, even if not entirely bowled over by Catholicism.

In a private session with Gary and me, the parish priest said to us, "It doesn't matter to me where the two of you worship after you are married, only that you worship together and create a spiritual environment for your children." The pastor made it clear that whether or not Gary ever chose to convert was not the matter of most importance. The pastor's words, his acceptance of Gary's non-Catholic history, affected Gary deeply. Though Gary never chose to convert to Catholicism and I never asked him to, he said he felt so welcomed at St. Timothy's, he gave his presence to the traditions and rituals so integral to my chosen faith.

In this photograph we are all sharing in the celebration of Amanda's First Communion—not as a family of Catholics, but simply as a family.

Season's Greetings from the Bird House
1990

Dear Friends:

Ah, yes, the fat man flies and the Birds' annual Christmas letter arrives in the mail again (as usual, just in time for the holidays). Another eventful year. If you've got a few minutes, we'd like to tell you about it.

We started 1990 with a new motor home—new to us, anyway—a 25-foot, 1975 Winnebago. So far we've taken one more trip for fun than to the repair shop. Ski trips, hunting trips and trips to Arivaca are all on our schedule for "Winnie."

Gary was on TV in January telling everyone how the Chicago Cubs were treating the Boys and Girls Club badly by cutting us out of concessions at their spring training games. Didn't do any good, but the interview and four seconds of airtime were a kick!

Our big ski trip this year was to Breckenridge. Grandma Joan Bird met us there and spent the days chasing Amanda, Andrew and Morgan—the precious daughter of some friends—around the condo. Amanda and Morgan both learned to ski.

Amanda was four in April, Andrew turned two in July and Gary was recently declared over the hill... What a wonderful year. We sincerely hope that yours was just as wonderful.

Dear Santa and Mrs. Claus,

Hi! I am Amanda. My little brother is named Andrew. We are both very good kids. No, Andrew has been bad because he hits me. I have been good. Only bring 4 presents for Andrew. He would like to have cars and trucks, Legos, an airplane to fly by itself.

I would like to get ice cream Barbie shop, bathtub Barbies, P.J. Sparkles, Baby Sparkles, bride Barbie, ballerina Barbie and new Barbie clothes. When I grow up I want some pink high heels, purple also.

Bye Santa,

Goodbye.

A M B

(As dictated to her mother)

The Joyful Mysteries

The sequence of events from the moment I arrived at St. Timothy's are jumbled in my memory. I remember going to Mass. I remember reaching the top of the steps leading out of the sanctuary and meeting Mike Haran, a fellow trial attorney and parishioner.

According to Mike, I told him Gary was scheduled to attend a meeting in one of the World Trade Center towers that morning. Mike vividly recalls leading me into a conference room where we could speak in private, although I have only a vague recollection of our conversation. What I remember most is Mike's willingness to take charge and be of service in any way possible.

Sometime later I went alone into the chapel to pray. As a "cradle Catholic" I grew up praying the Rosary. The Rosary is a string of beads Catholics use in prayer and meditation, similar to the prayer beads used by practitioners of Buddhism and Hinduism, except that the purpose of the Rosary is to reflect upon key events and mysteries in the lives of Jesus and his mother, Mary. These events traditionally fall under the headings of the *Joyful Mysteries,* those that follow the life of Jesus from conception to the beginnings of his ministry; the *Sorrowful Mysteries,* centering on the events surrounding Jesus's crucifixion; and the *Glorious Mysteries*, celebrating the Ascension of Jesus and the Assumption of Mary.

As I slid into a chair in the back row, I felt called to begin praying the Rosary. Since I hadn't brought one with me, I began counting through the sequence of prayers on my fingers: *the Apostles Creed, the Our Father, three Hail Marys, the Glory be to the Father...*

Coming to the end of the final prayer meant I also had come to the end of what I knew to do. The children were safe at school. My cell phone remained silent.

Again, my memory of that morning's chain of events is confused and hazy, but at some point one of the nuns, Sister Lyn Allvin, approached me and offered assistance.

She asked if I wanted her to pray with me and, in that one simple question, I knew my next step. Seeing I didn't have a Rosary, she went and found one for me.

We sat together in the chapel where I told her I did not want to pray the *Sorrowful Mysteries;* I preferred instead to pray and meditate over the joyous, miraculous beginnings of Jesus's life.

We prayed together in hushed voices, our fingers moving along the strings of beads, one prayer at a time.

I believe in God, the Father Almighty, Creator of Heaven and earth. I believe in Jesus Christ, His only Son, our Lord... I believe in the Holy Spirit... resurrection of the body... life everlasting... Thy will be done, on earth as it is in Heaven... as we forgive those who trespass against us... Holy Mary, Mother of God, pray for us sinners, now and at the hour of our death...As it was in the beginning, is now, and ever shall be, world without end. Amen.

With Sister Lyn beside me, I turned my thoughts to each of the *Joyful Mysteries* in turn: *the Annunciation,* the angel Gabriel's announcement to the virgin Mary that she would conceive the Son of God; *the Visitation,* Mary's visit to Elizabeth, a relative who is pregnant with the child who will become John the Baptist; *the Nativity,* the birth of Jesus; and *the Presentation,* denoting the day Mary and Joseph present the infant Jesus to God in the temple.

As I continued to say the Rosary, word upon word, mystery upon mystery— with Sister Lyn elaborating on each one—I felt my prayers begin to reach Gary wherever he was, bridging the distance between us. I don't know how to describe the experience except to say I could not have felt more connected to him in those moments had we been in each other's arms.

In the course of our meditation, Sister Lyn began to recite aloud to me the fifth and last of *Joyful Mysteries: the finding of Jesus in the temple.*

As the Bible story goes, when Jesus is twelve he goes with his parents to Jerusalem for the feast of the Passover. When the feast is over, Mary and Joseph head back to Nazareth, assuming Jesus is somewhere among their large traveling party. But at the end of the first day's journey, Jesus is nowhere to be found. His panicked parents return to Jerusalem to search for him. On the third day of his absence, they find him in the temple, intently talking with the teachers. Jesus is incredulous over his parents' concern about his whereabouts and their fear of losing him.

"Why were you searching for me?" he asks. "Did you not know that I had to be in my Father's house?"

8

On that morning, sitting in that chapel, I had no way of knowing whether Gary was alive or whether he was gone from us. The enormity of the tragedy I had witnessed unfolding on my television was beyond comprehension. Yet I knew with a kind of certainty I had never known before that Gary was within God's protection and doing whatever he was being called to do.

I prayed the words of the *Joyful Mysteries,* but with more earnestness and intention than I had ever done before. I didn't simply recite the words in my mind, I felt them deep in the center of my heart. In the midst of my prayers, I felt my connection to Gary, and to God, with more certainty and strength than ever before.

Sometime during those hours between arriving at the church and accepting Mike Haran's offer to drive me home in my car, I clearly remember saying to God: "I do not know how to get through this, handle this or fix this. I give it all to You. It is in Your hands." For the first time in my life, I let go of all my fears and uncertainty, looked beyond my pride and ego, and surrendered fully to the infinite wisdom and power of God. The peace I felt in that moment not only remained with me, but grew within me throughout the days that followed.

God was still with me. And so was Gary.

Many days would pass before I learned Mike was mistaken about which building Gary was in that morning. Yet I will be forever grateful for his mistake because it allowed me to hope. It spared me from the profound shock and grief of a sudden, unexpected loss. I didn't get a visit from military personnel telling me my husband was killed in action. A doctor didn't meet me in a hospital corridor to tell me he didn't survive a car accident. I did not even see the gaping hole in the North Tower where the first plane hit with the knowledge my husband was on one of those floors.

Because I believed Gary to be in the second tower, I believed he would come out of the wreckage alive. After all, Gary was a highly trained risk manager who would know how best to guide himself and others to a place with the highest probability of being rescued, if not escape serious injury altogether.

As the hours passed, every scene of rescuers pulling someone out alive kept my hope alive as well. I also was encouraged by reports that the human body could live for up to ten days without water. I believed Gary was somewhere under all the debris just waiting for help to arrive.

And then, finally, there were no more images of survivors at Ground Zero.

I received a phone call from my pastor, Father Dale Fushek.

"Are you and the children ready to recognize that Gary is never coming back?"

I knew my answer was "Yes." I knew because the feeling of hope I had held onto for so many days was gone. I felt hollow, like a reed.

By then, however, something stronger than hope was there to lift me up. By then I felt the full foundation of my faith beneath me and the loving embrace of my family, friends and community.

Please don't misunderstand me: nothing could have spared me the pain of grief, the aching desire for Gary's physical presence with me and our children. Knowing that my grief and my responsibility as my children's sole surviving parent were all I could manage, I let my colleagues take over my law practice while I devoted the next weeks to allowing grief to take me wherever it led. Friends and family came to my home to mourn and pray with me—in much the same way Jewish families "sit shiva" to mourn the loss of a loved one.

I rarely went out, because as Arizona's only 9/11 widow, I had become a recognizable figure overnight. Everyone I encountered wanted so much to help, to participate somehow in healing our national tragedy. Many wanted to touch me as though they found in me a tangible means to express their own deep sense of loss. While I understood their intention, their need, I didn't have the strength just then to be anything for anyone but myself and my children.

I wanted to sink into my grief and yet not allow it to pull me under. One day a friend called me on the phone, utterly hysterical over what had happened to Gary. Hysteria was one place I knew I could not afford to let grief take me. It could only isolate me, especially from my children. I didn't want to allow my emotions to spin out of control to the point where I could no longer be an anchor for them.

Still I didn't hide my tears from Amanda and Andrew. I never hesitated to cry in front of them. I wanted to be authentic in their presence. I didn't hold back the tears that came whenever I looked at the books Gary had left on the nightstand next to his side of our bed; or when I looked out the window to see someone other than Gary mowing our lawn for the first time; or when I removed Gary's toothbrush from its holder so that authorities in New York could use it to identify his DNA. At night I lay in bed and breathed in the scent of Gary's pillow. Weeks passed before I could bring myself to change the bed linens.

For the sake of my children, I did my best to preserve my health. I ate even though I wasn't hungry. After taking Amanda and Andrew to school each morning, I rested as much as I needed throughout the day. I took comfort in reading all the cards and letters that came in the mail. I gave voice to my emotions in my journal and in conversations with family and friends.

Most of all, I thought of Gary. My memories of him filled all the hollow spaces hope had left behind.

Family Album

Gary and I each brought dogs into our relationship. My parents didn't allow me to have pets when I was growing up in Chicago, so once I was living on my own in Phoenix, I bought a Bischon puppy I named Nikki, short for Dominique deDemaret. Gary contributed Taffy and Good Dog (aka G.D.) a mixed breed with long black hair and four white paws Gary took in as a stray. The dog had no tags and no collar, just a willingness to follow Gary home and anywhere Gary went from then on. I'd say Gary was a sort of canine Pied Piper except the attraction was mutual. Even in the videos Gary took after our children were born, he'd turn the lens from one of our babies to follow the dogs running after a ball or chasing each other around a tree.

Here's Gary just home from work, his little family so eager to be with him–and he with them. It will be awhile before he takes the time to change out of his dress shirt, slacks and favorite Johnston & Murphy shoes.

Home Movies

The birth sac hangs empty from Lil's uterus as she stands over her foal, gently cleaning it with her tongue. I train the lens on the newborn—chocolate-colored with a white face–in utter disbelief that in the two minutes it took me to go inside the house, leave a phone message for our veterinarian and return with the video camera, I missed the main event.

After serving as Lil's midwife for the delivery, Gary now divides his attention between Lil, her foal and our other horse Dani, who paces anxiously outside the corral, stopping now and then to stretch her chestnut colored neck through the bars of the railing to get a closer look at this creature who has just taken over her spot as the baby in our equine family. After a few minutes, Gary grows concerned that Dani's overtures toward the foal are becoming slightly aggressive, so he moves her to another corral.

Since a neighbor child first spotted Lil standing in the pasture with a birth sac hanging from her hind end, a crowd has been gathering on our driveway where they can see all the action. Some, including me, have never seen a mare give birth and we have a lot of questions. So as I'm filming I call out to Gary, our resident horse expert, for the answers.

"Can you tell if it's a boy or girl?" I ask.

"Not yet," he answers.

"When will it stand up, Gary?"

"Probably in the next thirty minutes."

The camera captures the foal's first clumsy attempts to stand. Each time its legs collapse and end up sprawled out in all directions.

Meanwhile the microphone picks up the sound of Gary's voice on the cell phone as he answers the call from the vet and gives her the news. Suddenly he comes into view as he kneels down next to the foal, lifts its tail to peek underneath and then respectfully backs out of the new mother's way.

"It's a girl," he announces.

More than thirty minutes pass, yet the foal still hasn't quite been able to stand. The sun is setting as a trusting Lil lets Gary scoop her filly up into his arms and carry her to a bed of hay that Amanda and Andrew have prepared in an adjoining stall. There, with just three minutes left on the video camera's battery, the foal gets to her feet. She stands wobbling on spindly legs that splay out in all directions and then makes her first instinctive efforts to be fed.

Gary is in his element, a gallery of onlookers present as he jokingly gives the filly instructions from the sidelines.

"Other end, other end," he coos. "Move farther back. You're going in the right direction. Keep going. Keep going. There you are. Now look under there. No, down…"

There's no missing the fact that Gary's already in love with this horse.

We have no way of knowing that in less than five months, Gary will be gone. Nor can we know now what a profound meaning this new life Gary has helped usher into the world—this filly soon to be named Caty Lu—will come to hold in one young woman's life.

Feast of St. Francis

*God Our Heavenly Father, You created the world to serve humanity's
needs and to lead them to You. By our own fault we have lost the beautiful
relationship which we once had with all your creation. Help us to see that
by restoring our relationship with You we will also restore it with all
Your creation. Give us the grace to see all animals as gifts from You and
to treat them with respect for they are Your creation. We pray for all animals
who are suffering as a result of our neglect. May the order You originally
established be once again restored to the whole world...*

– St. Francis of Assisi
From *Prayer for the Animals*

"Francis, go and repair my house which, as you can see, is falling into ruins."

In the story of the young preacher's life, St. Francis of Assisi hears the voice of
Jesus speak these words as he kneels in the Church of San Damiano. Francis takes
the words literally, first attempting to sell cloth from his wealthy father's shop to
supply the cost of repairing the church and later, after renouncing his father and
modeling his life after Jesus, restoring several ruined churches, laying the bricks
with his own hands.

In the Catholic faith, St. Francis is the patron saint of peace and of animals. One
story of his life has Francis defending a wolf against the townspeople who want to
kill it for decimating their flocks. Francis pleads with them to feed the wolf instead,
explaining that the wolf was only motivated by hunger.

Gary loved animals as much as anyone I ever knew. He grew up around animals.
As soon as he was old enough, he was up every morning at four o'clock to slop

the pigs and milk the cow, balancing himself on a one-legged stool. He could ride a horse practically from the time he could walk and I don't think there was ever a time in his life when he didn't own at least one dog. Most of the time he had two or three.

One of the dogs he brought into our marriage—G.D.—was a stray he found in the desert one day while helping the Jaycees set up their annual Halloween haunted house. Gary wouldn't think of leaving any dog to fend for itself.

He once rescued a baby chick and gave it to Amanda, just in time to bring it on a family trip to Lake Montezuma to go wakeboarding. He even took the chick (that Amanda named "Pinto") with us on the boat. Here is a picture of Gary from that trip, sitting in a lawn chair by the lake with the chick asleep on his stomach.

When the time came to choose a date for the Mass to celebrate Gary's new life apart from us, Andrew was the first to endorse October 4, the Feast of St. Francis—a celebration of life and a day of peace. Amanda and I agreed it was the perfect time.

After meeting with Father Dale to begin making the arrangements, I passed by the parish gift shop where I had noticed a statue of St. Francis just a day or so before. I remembered thinking at the time how much the statue of this balding man cradling three birds reminded me of Gary. This time I walked into the shop and bought it. It stands in my bedroom today and remains a source of joy.

Local newspapers reported that more than one thousand people were present at Gary's memorial celebration. I trust that is true. I know I felt the overwhelming presence of love. Amanda selected all the music and I chose the passages of scripture to be read. Among them were verses from the book of *Isaiah, Chapter 43:*

> *When you shall pass through the sea, I will be with you; and through the rivers, they shall not overwhelm you; when you walk through the fires, you shall not be burned; neither shall the flame kindle upon you...*

Bishop Thomas J. O'Brien attended and eight priests concelebrated the Mass before one of Gary's friends and his brother, Tom, took their turns at the lectern to share their memories.

As a final tribute to Gary and as a symbol of peace, we released several dozen white doves into the sky.

More than four years later, I was asked to address a parents' group at a Catholic high school on the subject of the messages of St. Francis. I stressed then as I have here: that I am not a theologian, only someone who embraces the mystery of faith and is willing to share my journey with anyone interested to know.

In studying the life and writings of St. Francis in preparation for my presentation that evening, two things stood out for me. One was the story of St. Francis relinquishing all his possessions. As punishment for wanting to spend all his money on the poor, Francis's father brought him to the courtyard of the bishop. There before the entire population of Assisi, the bishop demanded that Francis renounce all his possessions. Without hesitation, Francis stripped himself of his clothes, handed them to his father and stood naked for all to see.

The second was a line from what is known as *The Prayer of St. Francis:*
It is in pardoning that we are pardoned.

If my experience both before and after 9/11—both while Gary was with me and over the years since our last morning together—has taught me anything, it is that nothing is served by holding on to anger, resentment or any thoughts of retribution. Unless and until I am willing to "strip myself" of such negative feelings, unless and until I am willing to make the *choice to forgive*, I cannot be open and ready for the next gift God has for me.

We can never know in advance when we will be presented with that choice— when, like St. Francis, we will be faced with losing something we hold dear without bitterness and without giving up on our faith. St. Francis gave up his family identity, his reputation and his financial security without fear and without anger toward the bishop, his father—anyone. Both literally and symbolically, he let go of his former life and willingly surrendered to the mystery of God's plan for him.

I've come to believe that forgiveness, healing and the ability to live a peaceful, joy-filled life is all about maintaining a relationship with God. It is not my job to seek punishment for others. What is mine to do is to maintain my connection with God. That was the message contained in the first line of my doctor's "treatment plan":

And we know that in all things God works for the good of those who love Him, who have been called according to His purpose.

16

Family Album

Bobbi Holcomb and her younger sister Kristi lost both of their parents within nine months of each other —their father from a heart attack and their mother from cancer. Kristi and Amanda were best friends, and we considered the two sisters an extension of our family. During the summer our filly Caty Lu was born, Bobbi started coming over every morning to learn about horses from Gary. To say that the news of his death hit her hard does not begin to bear witness to the pain I saw in her. Sometime afterward, Bobbi was inspired to write about their friendship, so I think it fitting to let her share it in her own words, in the story she titled, The Summer of Gary.

On April 22, 2001, I heard Amanda Bird's voice on my sister Kristi's answering machine.

"Kristi! Dad's horse Lil just had her baby!" she said. "It's a girl and we named her Caty because she was born on your birthday." (Cathleen is my sister's middle name.) About a month later, I attended a belated birthday celebration for both

Kristi and Amanda. After a while I wandered out back to look at the baby horse. I had mentioned to Donna that, although I had always loved horses, I'd had few opportunities to work with them. She told me Gary loved being with people who appreciated the horses as much as he did and before the party was over, Gary had found me outside Caty's stall and invited me to come by any time to help with the chores, learn to ride or work with baby Caty.

Starting at six o'clock the next morning and every morning thereafter, I soaked up everything Gary had to teach. We ran into some trouble getting a halter on the filly and after readily admitting that patience wasn't his strongest suit, Gary gave me a sly grin and bet me five dollars I couldn't get a halter on Caty by the end of the week. I took his dare and agreed I'd have Caty wearing the halter by Friday. With that Gary went back to the house to get ready for work.

I'll never forget the mix of surprise, respect and pride on his face when he came out an hour later to find Caty in her brand new halter. I had passed the test. He returned to the house and came back with a five-dollar bill.

"Don't worry about the money," I told him.

"If I'm stupid enough to make the bet," he said, "I'm going to pay up." He laughed when I told him it was the first time I'd ever bet on a horse.

As I was about to leave for the morning, he came to me with his arms open wide and said, "I always give my kids a hug before they leave."

When I got home I tacked his five-dollar bill to my bulletin board. It's still there.

The next three weeks were some of the most fun and challenging of my life. While the horses were having their breakfasts and his family was still asleep, Gary and I sat in the kitchen, ate the bagels he toasted for us and read the newspaper. He would try to persuade me to buy stocks while I tried to persuade him to believe his horoscope. After breakfast came my lessons when my inexperience really showed. The day we took Caty on her first walk, she dragged me halfway up the street on my knees. Gary chuckled to see my ripped jeans and brought out the first aid kit.

I was riding Lil for my lesson on how to trot when she went under a pole, sending me somersaulting off her back. I lay on my back in the dirt looking up at Gary's silhouette standing over me.

"You okay?" he asked.

"Yes," I told him.

"Your pride okay?"

It ticked me off that he knew me so well.

The day he caught me singing to the filly, Gary asked me why I called her "Caty Lu."

"No reason," I answered. "It's her new nickname, that's all."

I had to say "goodbye" to Gary and the horses at the end of June when I left for a college study program in Italy. Gary gave me photos of Caty to take along with his assurances that she wouldn't forget me. Although I had a great time in Europe, I felt homesick for those mornings with Caty and Gary. I'm certain every other student on that trip got sick and tired of hearing about the filly I was learning to train. Jet lag and all, I was in the stalls my first morning back from Italy. When we went inside the house, Gary told me had something to show me. He produced a sheet of paper and told me he had officially registered Caty with the American Quarter Horse Association. I looked at the certificate and cried. Gary had given her the name "Bobbi's Caty Lu."

Over the following weeks, Gary continued to make a horsewoman of me. After months of making fun of my ripped jeans, he took me to a Western store to buy me some "good, sturdy work boots" and my first pair of Wrangler jeans.

As we climbed into the car with my new gear he turned to me and said, "Well, now you're an official cowboy. Welcome to the club."

I last saw Gary on Labor Day. When I got to the house that morning, he had already left, taking Dani to a trainer's facility. So Donna sat down in his place and ate a bagel with me as we talked about how the two of them had met and about what a strong, loving marriage they had. I told her that someday I wanted to find a guy whom Gary would approve of and that I wanted a marriage like theirs.

When Gary got home we shared a conversation like so many others we'd shared that summer. He told me about what a bad girl Dani had been at training that day and I told him about my classes and about the guy I was seeing.

When it was time for me to go, I told him I'd check my work schedule for the week and be over as soon as I could. As he stood by Dani and watched me walk down the driveway, I turned and said, "Bye, Gary. I'll see you one of these days."

And that was all.

All I know about horses is what Gary taught me, so I don't know whether horses cry. All I know is that in the days after that terrible September 11, something has left streaks down the sides of Caty's face. I see them every morning.

I do the best I can with Gary's babies, though I struggle to figure out what he would want me to do.

Out in the pasture, with the dew on the grass and the sun peeking over the rooftops, I sing to Caty and I thank Gary for teaching me about horses, about myself, about unconditional love and about enjoying every moment. And I thank him for leaving me a piece of himself in Caty.

Don't worry, Gary. I'll take care of her like you took care of me.

Home Movies

For many years, Gary's mother, Joan (pronounced Jo-ann), spent her winters working as a caretaker for the Saguaro Lake Ranch Resort forty miles east of Phoenix, at the base of the Stewart Mountain Dam. When winter was over, she loaded up her green van and drove to her summer job at another ranch in Wyoming. Gary and I, along with extended family members, liked to visit Joan at the ranch resort, especially during the Christmas holidays. The year she was born, we brought Amanda with us, along with that video camera we were still learning how to use. Gary did all the filming and narration. The scenery, if not the cinematography, was worthy of any John Ford western—the kind of place where Gary was in his element.

I'll let Gary tell you, in his own words, some of what he saw through the camera lens:

> As we come around to the right, we see the entrance to Saguaro Lake. Coming around a little bit farther, we get a panorama of the Bulldogs, some massive rock formations just across the Salt River from the entrance to the ranch. The houses in the foreground are the homes for the people who work at the dam.
>
> Here we are at the ranch and here's the tail end of a small group of people coming back from a [trail] ride...
>
> There's the lodge and the eating area. You can see the cabins off to the left. As we come around, you can see a few more of the cabins, some of the large trees, a large open area, stone fence and down to the road we came in on, with the Bulldogs behind. Up in one of those hills is a nest of bald eagles...

Gary makes a point of calling attention to the flower bed his mother planted just outside the lodge and to the Santa Claus decoration on the front porch. He walks over to the corrals where Joan and I are introducing Amanda to horses for the first time. The lens zooms in on Amanda until her image fills the screen.

> Hi, Amanda. Hi, Baby. Hi, Sweetie. There she is...

So much for John Ford. So much for capturing in words and images the scenic wonders of Saguaro Lake. Nothing in the world captivated Gary more than his children.

Boots

It's about making sure that the horses, cows, dogs and people are safe, no matter what's going on. It's about love. It's about being a cowboy.

– Rocco Wachman, from *Cowboy*

As Gary was packing for his business meetings in New York City, he jokingly asked whether he should wear his cowboy boots. I smiled and told him I advised against it.

"Even if I take off the spurs?" he responded with a wink.

He mentioned his decision to leave the boots behind to his friend and colleague Jonathan Russell when their paths crossed at the airport as Gary headed for his flight. The reason he gave Jonathan?

You can't give them too much of a good thing too soon.

Although throughout his professional life, Gary outfitted himself in suits, ties and dress shoes, he was most comfortable in cowboy boots and a pair of Wrangler jeans. Gary was a cowboy born and raised. He logged many hours on horseback even while still in the womb, as his mother Joan continued to ride through her eighth month of pregnancy. By the age of three, he could shinny up a horse's leg, grab hold of the mane and swing himself onto its back. Joan remembers glancing out her kitchen window to see her toddler on horseback and wondering how on earth he got there.

Dan, like the son he raised, was a man most at home on a horse under an open sky. Unlike Gary, however, he never wore anything but a cowboy hat, Western shirt, boots, and the Wrangler jeans that couldn't conceal a butt as flat as a mesa.

About eight years after Gary was born in Cottonwood, Arizona, his father Dan moved the family to an eighty-acre farm outside of Pea Green, Colorado, a town with one grocery store, one gas station and a small community center—all at the same intersection. Gary attended grade school in the one-room schoolhouse nearby. He attended the first two years of high school seven miles away in Olathe, a farming community known for its fields of sweet corn, and graduated from Mohave County Union High School in Kingman.

Downtown Kingman, Arizona, circa 1968, as it
appeared in Gary's high school yearbook.

Gary was Dan and Joan's middle child, arriving between son Tom and adopted daughter Diane. Half-sister Penny—Dan's daughter from his first marriage—lived with them. Gary was a teenager when his parents' marriage ended in divorce. Dan remarried shortly before I came into the picture, and he and Helen were still happy together when Dan passed away in 1993.

In temperament, Gary grew up to be like his father: gentle, loving, wise and strong with the heart and soul of a true cowboy, a breed whom author and television personality Rocco Wachman describes this way in his book, *Cowboy:*

> *He is honorable, trustworthy, polite, deliberate, displays etiquette and good manners, and is well dressed and manicured when in public. He is also a romantic by nature, and an enigma to most who do not live in his world. He represents the yin and yang, the good and the bad, depending on the situation at hand. And he is, first and foremost, a gentleman—unless duty obligates him to act otherwise.*

Those words describe Gary and his father to a "T."

Dan Bird also raised his son to be an early riser who took care of his responsibilities without complaint. He taught Gary that whatever a person sets out to do, they should set out to do it right and do it right every time.

Where the two of them diverged, however, was in the area of business. Dan thought of himself as an entrepreneur. Over the years, he embarked on a series of ventures—including investing in windmills—and although he worked very hard to be successful, his enterprises ultimately failed.

In contrast, colleagues referred to Gary as a "corporate cowboy" in the sense that he was as proficient in a corporate setting as he was riding the range. For Gary, however, working for a big corporation was only the means to one end: the ability to support a family before retiring to his own eighty-acre spread where he could serve as a trail guide for others longing for wide open spaces. Until that day came, he satisfied his cowboy nature with an acre of pasture land we bought in Tempe where Gary got up early every morning to go feed and talk to the horses he referred to as "his girls."

Gary was working in risk management for the Phelps Dodge Corporation when he came up with an unorthodox plan for mixing business with one of his greatest pleasures: invite his "stable" of insurance underwriters on a trail ride. To help him put his plan into action, he turned to friend and colleague Mike Goss, a broker with Marsh USA who by then handled three-quarters of the account connected with the Phelps Dodge Corporation's mining operations. Although most brokers did their best to prevent any fraternization between clients and underwriters, Gary knew Mike would see things differently. Like Gary, Mike was a third-generation Arizonan who grew up riding horses and believing in the principle that a man's word is his bond— what Mike refers to as "the code of the West." The biggest difference between the two men was that, in Mike's words, "I was more into my career than into horses, and Gary only had a career to enable him to ride horses."

Yet it came as no surprise to Mike when Gary told him he wanted to spend time with every agent involved in the fates of mine workers and their families. Mike remembers Gary telling him: "I want to stare him in the eye. I want to shake his hand and get to know him."

Mike agreed to fund the inaugural trail ride, putting up twelve-hundred dollars from his company's small entertainment budget to cover the cost of food, beverages and other supplies, as well as compensate Gary's father, Dan, for his services in setting up camp and acting as the official "sourdough" (otherwise known as "camp cook").

The first annual Gary Bird trail ride for insurance brokers and underwriters was a no-frills affair. Mike and the half-dozen city slickers in attendance slept in tents, while Gary and Dan slept outside on tarps spread out on the ground. Dan contributed his own horses plus a few he borrowed from friends. He and Gary taught each man how to saddle his own horse before the day's ride and, twenty to thirty miles later at trail's end, how to brush the horse down and check the hooves. Sitting around a campfire drinking beer and swapping stories—although no business, please—rounded off the day's activities.

But as the tradition and the attendance grew, so did the accommodations and the entertainment. For subsequent trips, Gary and Mike made reservations at small ranches around Arizona that supplied the horses and where there were bunkhouses—with real beds. They not only hired a full-time cook, but also arranged for a banjo player and a cowboy poet to spice up the evening campfires.

Mike loves to tell the story about the night he and Gary sat by the campfire long after everyone else had gone to sleep. Gary was never much of a drinker, but on this particular night he and Mike managed to over-whet their whistles and just before turning in for the night, Gary magnanimously gave Mike the entire Phelps Dodge account.

"I'll never forget the look on his face the next morning when he realized what he had done," Mike says. "I'm sure he never forgot the look on mine when he took it back."

Although Ric Glover, an underwriter at the Marsh office in Phoenix, was among those who enjoyed the benefit of a mattress on his first trail ride experience, what he most remembers was how sore he felt as he eased himself off his horse at the end of every day. His pain was shared by his colleagues from New York who left their cushy office chairs to park their behinds on a saddle for hours at a stretch, for three to four straight days.

As Ric remembers it, "Gary was a big enough customer that when he invited them to go on a trail ride, they were pretty much obligated to say 'Yes.'"

Yet Ric also remembers that by the end of every trip, even the greenest among them had caught the cowboy spirit. Some even signed up for riding lessons almost as soon as their planes touched down back in the city.

Gary's love for horses was not only contagious, it was selfless and unconditional. One scorching hot morning while talking to our neighbor and fellow horse lover, Deb Keller, over the metal fence separating our two properties, Gary looked at the barren corrals behind our house and lamented over the lack of shade trees. He wasn't missing the shade for himself, mind you, but for his horses.

After Gary died, in lieu of flowers or other remembrance, Deb and her husband bought an oak tree and planted it in the middle of our pasture. One way or another, Gary always managed to get his horses whatever they needed.

Ironically, the neighbors who settled in across the road from us in Tempe—Jack and Prudence—moved to Arizona from New York to try their hand at the cowboy life for the first time. Jack still likes to talk about all the hours Gary worked to "cowboy him up." On the eighth anniversary of the WTC attacks, they posted a letter on the Internet. Along with their memories of watching Gary through their kitchen window for weeks on end as he patiently trained one of his horses, they wrote:

> *We moved to Arizona thinking that buying a ranchette and quarter horses was a great idea. Fortunately for us, Gary lived across the street and was kind and patient enough to point out the difference between the front and back ends of a horse. He broke us in for two years and we still care for the same horses with the understanding and love for these animals that Gary imparted to us.*

Before Gary left for New York, he mentioned to me that he felt "a little scared." I attributed his comment to the initial jitters that come with any new job. I commented lightly that his departure was a bit like going off to kindergarten.

In retrospect, however, I believe there was a bit more to the anxiety he was feeling. In 1984, I accompanied him to New York City for a convention of the Risk and Insurance Management Society (RIMS). Three days into the four-day trip, Gary told me he felt claustrophobic in that "city of concrete walls." The Chicago girl that I am, I didn't understand and asked him to explain why.

"Because I can't see the horizon," he said.

After the 1993 bombings at the World Trade Center, Gary shared with a colleague his belief that terrorists would one day target the site again and with even more devastating results. The risk manager in him saw the World Trade Center as a vulnerable, risky place to be. In light of their conversation, his colleague assumed Gary would never put himself there.

And yet when the opportunity to serve arose in the form of a new job, he went willingly to a place that made him feel uncomfortable, even "a little scared." Our daughter Amanda says she knew from the moment we heard that both towers had been hit that her father spent his last seconds on earth helping to save others. He was, after all, a cowboy:

> *Among [the cowboy's] qualities are an adventurous soul that finds great joy in facing the unknown, a never say quit attitude that overcomes any obstacle, a free spirit that allows him to roam the land wherever he believes destiny leads him, a ruggedness that almost gladly accepts and conquers the hardships life bestows upon him, an unquestionable faith in himself and the men with whom he works and depends on for survival, and an inner strength that allows him to forge ahead when all odds are stacked against him.*

– Rocco Wachman, from *Cowboy*

Gary and his favorite horse, Lil, took the lead on many trail rides in their time together. On a sunny November morning in 2001, Lil helped lead nearly sixty riders from Tempe and surrounding communities on a ride held to honor Gary's memory. The ride began at Tempe Town Lake and proceeded along a trail that winds through the red rocks of Tempe's Papago Park. Gary's saddle was on Lil's back and his boots were in the stirrups, but the saddle was empty and the boots faced backward—a tradition that has come to represent a fallen rider taking one last look back at his family. Amanda, Andrew and I rode along with the group, behind Lil. I could almost see Gary sitting there and smiling; one of my favorite photographs had always been the one of him on horseback, playfully facing the wrong way.

Gary's cowboy spirit continued to touch people long after he was gone. On the first anniversary of 9/11, a man named Michael Browers from Woodland Hills, California, posted this letter on the Internet:

Yesterday, 11 September 2002, I had the privilege of participating in one of the many events honoring those who tragically lost their lives on 9/11. The event in which I participated was a motorcycle ride held here in southern California. Each motorcyclist rode for one of the victims. I rode for Gary Bird.

We were presented with a list of names from which to choose. For some reason, as I reviewed the long list of names, Gary's seemed to jump off the page at me. I had thought it was because he was from Tempe, where I had studied architecture at ASU. Or maybe it was his age, the same as mine. In any case, I chose Gary as my person to honor, all the while feeling there was something more to this choice, but not understanding what it might be.

Now some may think that motorcycle riders are just of bunch of loud, crazy people getting together for a good time (and frequently that is the case). But for me, this was my way of honoring someone in my own special way. I was part of a contingent of motorcycles, many of which were ridden by firefighters and police officers from southern California. The ride was escorted by fire trucks and various police vehicles, and ended at a memorial tribute to the victims of 9/11. During the ride and memorial I spent my time thinking about this man, Gary, whom I had selected to carry with me. I wondered what it was that drew me to this person, what he was like, about his family, about that tragic day one year ago.

I carried Gary in my heart the entire day and into the night, strangely touched by someone I did not know.

Today I found this site on the web and was able to learn something about this person who so deeply, and unexpectedly, touched my life. Then I understood, at least in part. My wife and I are both horse people, and when I read of Gary's passion for horses I knew that this was the unexpected

26

connection. Our horses are part of our family and integral to our lives, our
emotions, and our outlook and approach to life. And anyone who understands
this about horses will understand my connection with Gary.

I was privileged to honor Gary, if only in a small, insignificant way. He
and his family will be in my heart for the rest of my life, and every time I ride
my horse, Gary will ride with me.

On September 7, 2002, I flew to New York City, accompanied by a family member, to retrieve the ashes of what little was found of Gary's remains and to attend a luncheon given by Marsh USA as a tribute to the 252 employees who lost their lives at the World Trade Center. I had declined to know exactly what searchers found and what medical examiners had identified as my husband. Instead, I gave officials permission to share that information with Father Dale.

We flew into the city on a cloudless, radiant afternoon, but the next day as we drove through the streets of Manhattan, I noticed for the first time how the buildings stood as a fortress against the light, against anything outside their borders. For the first time, I felt as Gary had: confined and longing for space. Yet I took comfort in knowing that I was joining Gary in the place he last lived, where a part of him would always be. I tried to imagine the joy he must have felt on that radiant Sunday morning in September as he left our house and set out to begin his dream job.

The children and I chose to bury Gary's ashes in Phoenix's St. Francis cemetery with an uninterrupted, 360-degree view of the horizon. I kept his spurs, which hang near the pair his father wore over the kitchen window that looks out on his idea of heaven.

His boots, we buried with him.

Being a cowboy isn't about roping calves, riding bulls, or polishing off a fifth of Jim Beam. Being a cowboy is a mind set that permeates everything the cowboy is and does. It is a mental toughness that sees in every hardship a challenge to overcome the impossible, and it is having a presence that demands the highest level of respect and that offers even more respect in return. It is about knowing when to be self reliant and when to team up with others to battle the situation at hand. It is about caring for the land, animals, and the people you love, and it is about leaving the world better off than how you found it. That's what being a cowboy is all about.

– Rocco Wachman, from *Cowboy*

Family Album

The front of the T-shirt reads "BIRDSHI(R)T"and is decorated with ribbons of simulated bird...poo. The shirt was token of good-natured affection specially made for the occasion of Gary being named a "senator," the highest international honor that may be granted to a member of the United States Junior Chamber, otherwise known as the Jaycees. The year was 1985 and the honor—the most recent in a series awarded to him—came after more than twenty years with the organization, first as the chairman in charge of organizing swim meets for community children and later as Director, Secretary, Vice President, President and Chairman of the Board.

As the newly-appointed senator's wife, I was presented with a Birdshi(r)t of my very own. I once teased Gary that were we ever to divorce, I would be happy to leave all the bird-themed memorabilia to him.

And yet here it is ten years since he left us and I still have those shirts.

A Letter of Thanksgiving
From the Birds
November, 2001

Dear Family and Friends,

We wanted to send this letter expressing our profound appreciation to the hundreds of people who have been with us through the weeks since the devastating tragedy of September 11th. It's very hard to put into words how much comfort we have derived from the cards, personal letters, calls, photos, visits, books, gifts of food and more. The level of our appreciation cannot be quantified; it is immense. The peace brought by your thoughts, prayers and hugs is palpable and embracing; we feel it every day, all day long.

Without each and every one of the people who either expressed their love openly, or quietly felt it in their hearts, we would never have made it through this most difficult time. A deep and abiding faith has been the other element in our progress toward a sense of peace about the loss of our beloved husband and father. I thank God, and each of you, so very much.

October 3, 2001

Dear Donna:

My deepest sympathies for you
and your family on the tragic
passing of Gary. He was a fine
man, good father, great husband,
nice guy — everything you want
and admire in a human.

The solace you have is that
he lived his life to the fullest, with
zeal, zest and appreciation for
all that is good.

Respectfully
Rod

Instruments of Peace

It was the people. They were all responsible for the life that was restored to our undernourished orphan, for giving it the strength to survive and flourish in the East Valley. A few believed and never gave up, then others began to believe! Finally, like a Phoenix bird rising out of the ashes, the Boys and Girls Club of Tempe, with the help of the many, returned from the brink of financial ruin to show a community its true worth.

Gary penned those words for an article he was asked to write in the spring of 1986. In those few opening lines, he mentioned so many of his core values: children, community, strength, belief and the power of never giving up. *It was the people. They were responsible for the life that was restored...*

The article that ran in a small quarterly issue of *Arizona Parks and Recreation* told the story of some selfless men and women who volunteered their time and resources in saving the organization dedicated to providing a safe, productive and nurturing place for children to gather. Gary made no more than a brief reference to the person who took out a personal loan to pay the staff salaries, but that's because he didn't want anyone to know he was the one who paid them—with his credit card.

Gary was always most comfortable behind the scenes of any production. He was fairly new to the Tempe Jaycees when he offered to assist the organization's president, John "Hut" Hutson, meet a somewhat unusual request from the city's mayor: *Take over the responsibility of the annual Christmas display at the top of Tempe Butte.*

Tempe Butte is one of the city's most recognizable landmarks, located adjacent to Arizona State University's Sun Devil Stadium. At the start of each academic year, a group of ASU students make the annual trek up the winding face of the butte to put a fresh coat of gold paint on the giant letter "A" that honors their school. (Visiting rival schools have been known to sneak up there at night to repaint the hallowed symbol with their own school colors.)

Sometime in the 1930s, the City of Tempe began the holiday season tradition of erecting a lighted star and three camels that could be seen for miles. Whether for lack of funds or personnel willing to do the work of carrying on the tradition, the mayor approached Hut in 1985 with the idea of turning the project over to the Jaycees. Hut agreed and Gary stepped forward to help him organize the group they dubbed "Friends of Tempe Butte."

Satisfied, the mayor turned over to the group, not the prefabricated star and camels, but merely a set of plans for how to construct their own. Hut arranged for inmates at the state prison in Florence to do the construction for four-thousand dollars, after which he and Gary mobilized the campaign to earn the money back.

On the pre-appointed day, thirty Jaycees showed up to help transport and assemble the decorations. Each camel came in three sections of marine plywood that, when assembled, stood more than eighteen feet tall. The star came in five sections, the last of which had to be hoisted into place using a block and tackle. Thankfully the original concrete and metal braces for the giant camel processional were still firmly rooted in the ground, but that's all the guidance the group had to go on. For Hut, the scene was reminiscent of a comedy performance by two famous ice skaters from the 1940s who were forever falling and running into each other.

"We were like Frick and Frack," Hut remembers. "Of course it didn't help anything that we drank beer all day. We learned after that first year that you don't drink until you get them up the hill and put together."

Gary had begun his service with the Tempe Jaycees by organizing swim meets for community children. The welfare of children was always closest to his heart. Before we had children of our own, Gary invited a boy from the Tempe Boys and Girls Club on the Jaycees' annual "father and son" camping trip. No one asked him to. He did it because, to use Hut's words, "It was just Gary's way."

Gary closed his article about the Tempe Boys and Girls Club with these words: *Visit the Tempe Boys and Girls Club sometime. See the beaming faces and hear the laughter of the children as they enjoy the fruits of the labors of a very special community. The people were there for us then and we are there for them now.*

Gary knew and believed in the profound impact one person can have in the lives of others, but it wasn't until the days following his death that I came to fully realize that impact for myself.

One evening just a week after the terrorist attacks, I was sitting in St. Timothy's Catholic Community listening to a presentation by an author who had recently published a book about Pope John Paul II when I "heard" a voice instruct me to open my copy of the book and, inside the front jacket, write the words, "Instrument of Peace." I couldn't recall ever having received a spiritual message with such clarity. Nevertheless, I wrote the words in pencil in case it turned out I wasn't spiritually inspired, just loony.

Following the presentation, Father Dale led us in prayer for the victims of the terrorist attacks. Then he invited me to join him at the altar so that the hundreds of people gathered there could pray over me.

With the pastor's arm around my shoulders and tears running down my face, my church community stood before me with their arms extended and offered their outpouring of prayers. When it was over, Father Dale handed me the microphone. As the room fell silent I did something entirely out of character as a trial attorney who rarely speaks without carefully weighing every word beforehand. Without hesitation I uttered the words, "I still love the Lord."

As extraordinary as the events of that evening felt to me at the time, their full power and meaning would unfold gradually over the months and years to come, revealed to me by the countless instruments of peace who reached out to me and my family.

Cards and letters came by the hundreds. People I knew only in passing wrote to express their feelings of sadness and offer their support. I heard from a couple I had often encountered at the restaurant I frequented on Saturday mornings. A colleague sent me a copy of a poem her son planned to read the next day at his Bar Mitzvah, with all the families of the lost in mind. The owner of the shoe repair shop we'd been coming to for years sent his condolences. He later told me he had doubted I would ever come into his shop again because he was born in Baghdad. He thought I might blame him somehow.

Girls from Amanda's former Brownie Troop 1419 made us a quilt—one of five handmade quilts we received, including a blue and white patchwork from a stranger in Andrew, Iowa, and a crocheted replica of the American flag a neighbor and her husband carried to our front door one cold, very rainy evening. A senior English class at Leona High School in New Jersey chose Gary to honor, displaying his picture on their classroom door under the words, *You will always be in our hearts.*

A little boy I had never met sent me a little cross he cut out of fabric and all the money he had to give—forty-one cents—all packaged in a plastic Halloween treat bag.

A woodworker sent a case to hold an American flag.

Strangers from my community, from all over the country, sent their condolences. Their letters all opened with some variation of *You don't know me, but...*

Dear Donna,

I've never written to someone I didn't know before, but I've felt compelled to let you know that I'm continuing to pray for you and your family during this very tragic time...

Dear Mrs. Bird and Family,

I would like to express my deepest sympathy to you and your family in this time of grief and sadness.

I do not know you personally, but I felt led by God to let you know your situation has touched my heart. I am from New York and have family that was just blocks away from the devastation that took your husband's life. While they returned home, I am saddened that your husband did not...

I opened cards from President George W. Bush, Vice President Cheney, Senator John McCain from Arizona and New York Mayor Rudy Giuliani.

However one letter will always stand out, not because it came with any more compassion or sincerity than the rest, but because, in a way, it came from Gary:

Dear Donna,

My prayers, along with those of so many, have been with you through the tragedy of losing Gary. The memorial service was a beautiful tribute to his life, but the best tributes are the memories of how he touched all of us individually while he was with us.

Gary was a hero in life, as well as in death. The way he lived his life was an example of kindness and true generosity. He made sure that all of our business transactions were fair for both of us and never wanted to take advantage of our relationship. He always went the extra mile in so many ways, like offering the use of your place in Purgatory after we talked about our mutual love of skiing. He didn't ask for, nor did he expect, anything in return. In death, he will continue to be an example, showing us the impact each of us can have on others by living our lives as selflessly as he did.

At the end of August, Gary called me and asked me to find out if there was anything you might like for Christmas. I called the Tempe store to see if anything had caught your eye. My manager told me that Gary wanted to get this gift for you. Merry Christmas, from your husband Gary.

In Jesus Christ our Lord,

Jim Chase
Ganem Jewelers

Enclosed with the letter was a box containing a pair of opal earrings.

Many people wrote to share their own personal stories of loss and of the journey through grief that brought healing and peace. A woman from my parish wrote about her husband's sudden, unexpected death while playing a game of tennis, leaving her to finish raising three daughters under the age of seventeen. "[Call] if you would like to talk and need a listener," she wrote. "I have not walked the mile in your shoes but I have survived and worn out a few pair of shoes along my own journey to recovery with my children."

Another woman shared the experience of losing her husband after eighteen months of cancer treatments.

"I still can't believe he won't walk in the door, but as I go about what I need to do, I realize life is different now," she wrote. "How people can go on without a strong faith, I do not know."

People sent poems, words of Scripture—one sent a CD of Andrea Bocelli singing *The Prayer*—anything that had helped them through their own times of grieving. Many simply offered the solace of knowing that pain does lessen with time:

> *We lost our nineteen-year-old daughter with no warning five and a half years ago… At the time, a friend who had been widowed a few years earlier said to us, "Time is your friend." She was correct.*

Many cards contained money to support Amanda and Andrew's education or Gary's work in the community.

One of those donations came from the Suzanne Maria Rossetti Memorial Scholarship Fund. I never met Suzanne Rossetti; I represented her parents in a lawsuit against the State of Arizona. It was my first big case as an attorney just two years out of law school.

Standing five feet tall and weighing a hundred pounds, Suzanne, a vivacious brunette, was the youngest of Peter and Louise Rossetti's three children. After graduating from an eastern university, she moved to Arizona where her parents had purchased a vacation home in Scottsdale. She became an avid hiker and rock climber and, while she made the best of her job processing pig skin for treating severe burn victims, she was looking forward to being promoted to the marketing position that would allow her to move to New York, closer to family.

On the night of January 28, 1981, Suzanne stopped at a convenience store, inadvertently locking the keys inside her car. Her mistake provided the perfect opportunity for two men looking to score some cash. One of these men was Michael David Logan, a career criminal who had escaped from a Michigan prison. The other was Jesse James Gillies, convicted of rape as a juvenile in California and later of felony theft following an incident in which he assaulted a mentally challenged man outside of Phoenix.

Had the probation officer assigned to Gillies read the file carefully enough to know Gillies was already on probation in California; had the Arizona Department of Corrections adhered to the plea agreement Gillies signed in the assault case, requiring that he serve one year in county jail; had Gillies not been transferred to a halfway house due to prison overcrowding; had prison authorities followed the recommendations of two officers who independently recommended his work-release pass be rescinded because of his incorrigible attitude and behavior; Gillies would not have been free to encounter the perfect accomplice in Michael David Logan, and the pair would not have been waiting in the convenience store parking lot the night Suzanne Rossetti stopped to buy a pack of gum. Were it not for the careless negligence of prison authorities and the vicious, unfeeling nature of those two men, Suzanne Rossetti would not have been abducted, robbed, repeatedly raped and beaten. She would not have been tossed over the side of a mountain road, her skull crushed with a rock, and left to die.

At the time I met Suzanne's parents, I had no experience with such unimaginable violence against someone I loved, no experience with such a tragic loss. I couldn't tell them I knew that kind of pain. I couldn't even share in any memories of their daughter since I had never met her. The best I could do was support them in my professional capacity as an attorney and assist them in holding the authorities charged with public safety accountable for their blatant failures.

When I lost Gary to an act of senseless violence, the Rossetti family reached out to me. With the court settlement they were awarded from the state of Arizona, along with donations received at the time of their daughter's death, the Rossettis established the Suzanne Maria Rossetti Memorial Foundation to provide college scholarships to needy students from the high school Suzanne once attended in Massachusetts. Shortly after Gary's death, I received a card signed by Louise Rossetti, Suzanne's mother, and Peter Rossetti, Jr., Suzanne's older brother. The card was to let me know that Louise had made a contribution in Gary's name to her daughter's memorial scholarship fund and to a second fund created later in her husband's memory. Along with their kind generosity, the Rossetti family gave me something I was unable to give to them: the unspoken connection and understanding that comes from shared experience. I received this letter from Louise, from this woman who knew the pain of such a violent loss:

Donna, Andrew & Amanda:

I must apologize for not calling or writing you but I was hoping for a miracle when my niece sent me a copy of the newspaper...GARY WAS MISSING...I could not believe, suppose like you, was in a state of shock— hoping and praying it was not so...

This was the tragedy of this century and I regret that I did not write sooner BUT...there's that BUT again...procrastination...and no doubt you are just about becoming accustomed to the fact that he will never be...I know how difficult that is...and here I am, opening old wounds...mea culpa...

I so enjoyed our visit to your home when you were still bride and groom and you made delicious strawberry soup as the first course! I can't remember the main course but that strawberry soup was a new one for me and Peter... delicious...Peter said we should try making fruit soups if they taste as good as yours...of course, I never did—was never a good cook.

Gary was a wonderful husband and a great father and I know this because of your grand letters, especially your Christmas one and the pictures—Two Birds in a Tree—the children all dressed up in their 'Sunday go to meeting clothes'...among the many I taped to my kitchen wall photo gallery with many photos...just removed them...

Donna, you have lost a wonderful husband and we have lost a dear and good friend...I felt I really knew Gary because of your wonderful letters. You were like extended family...enjoying your great adventurous trips.

I can only offer my deepest sympathy at this time. I will keep you and the children in my prayers that God will grant you the strength and stamina to carry on as Gary would want. I'm sure his soul is in heaven and he will help you—like "Gary, where did we put it?"

You have many great memories—so do I and that's a plus when things seem to be troublesome. BUT YOU ALL WILL SURVIVE AND BE THERE FOR EACH OTHER. I love you all.

Love and peace,

Louise

A decade later I can look at Louise's words and know them to be true. No matter what life brings, we will all survive and be there for each other. We'll survive *because* we are there for each other.

———————

Little Gary is quiet tonight. There is no triptripping of little feet across the floor, into the kitchen and up on a chair where he looks up into my face and says, "Hi, Mama Bird. Me help you."

It used to be just "Mama." Then he got in the habit of going around the table calling us each by name: Daddy, Mama, Tommy, Penny (which he balled into such a knot, it could have been anything). Once he learned "Bird" he added it to all our names.

Little Gary is quiet tonight. I don't hear "Drink, Mama Bird," or "Butter Sandwich, Mama Bird," or "Shut up, Tommy Bird," or "You quit...No fair."

———————

(from a collection of reflections written by Joan Bird, 1952)

Gary E. Bird

The Intensive Care Nursing Staff
St. Mary's Hospital
1601 W. St. Mary's Road
Tucson, AZ 85745

Re: **Dan S. Bird - Patient Between March 5 and March 12**

Dear Nursing Staff:

Dan Bird was placed in your loving care on March 5, 1993 following a cardiac arrest which occurred while being treated for pneumonia in your hospital. He had suffered from the effects of a stroke for more than eighteen months and the "bouts" with pneumonia, among other problems, were becoming more frequent. The care you provided him during his stay with you and the concern you showed for his family are very much appreciated.

We find it difficult to imagine how you do your hard work every day with the critically injured, desperately ill and the dying. We are, however, inexpressibly grateful that you were there to do your work for Dan Bird in such a loving and caring manner.

Dan Bird died just a few hours after being removed from the systems being used to sustain his life. If he had been able, I'm sure that he would have told you how unexpectedly warm and gentle all of you are and how wonderfully you treated him during his last hours. We thank you.

With kindest personal regard,

for The Family of Dan S. Bird

Family Album

For our first Christmas together as husband and wife, Gary and I decided the most practical choice in a Christmas tree was an artificial one we found on sale for $200. We both much preferred a fresh tree, but those are pricey in Arizona. We calculated that by keeping the artificial tree for ten years, we could keep the annual cost down to $20, and by that time we could afford to buy a fresh tree every year.

Here you see Gary lifting Andrew so he can place the angel on top of the tree. If you look closely, you can see a couple of bird-shaped ornaments—a tradition started by Gary's Aunt Grace, but one I adopted. Every year I bought two new bird ornaments for our own Bird family tree.

Gary and I put up that artificial tree for every one of the nineteen Christmases we spent together. It became a running joke between us. Each holiday as we unpacked the box containing the increasingly decrepit conifer and set it up in the living room, one of us would turn to the other and ask, "What's our cost down to now?"

Neither of us would have traded that tree for anything.

(Gary wrote out this will before leaving on a business trip early in our marriage)

I, GARY BIRD, being of sound mind, do hereby declare this to be my
LAST WILL and TESTAMENT.

To my Father, Dan S. Bird, I leave all my firearms and hunting equipment. My
share of those parcels of land we share jointly shall also be his. All monetary
obligations are forgiven. I ask only that he expedite the sale of my 20 ac. parcel
and recover the $14,000 invested in the commercial building so that Donna,
my wife, can benefit from the proceeds.

To my mother, Joan M. Bird, I leave $500 and the love of a son. I would ask
that my wife, Donna, insofar as it is possible, accord my mother the same love,
consideration and hospitality as will be given to Gertrude in their late years.

To my sister, Diane, I leave $500 to help her on her way to a fun and fruitful
adult life for which she has struggled so long.

To my brother, Tom Bird, I leave my 1978 Ford Van. It is a useful though
gluttonous vehicle and Tom may do with it as he wishes.

To my sister, Penny Strange, and her family I leave my skiing and scuba diving
equipment. Keith or Dan may be able to use some of it.

To these and to my Grandmothers, Aunts and Uncles, cousins and the wonderful
family of my wife, Donna, I leave my love, respect and my best wishes for a
happy life.

To my friend, Doug Lyle, my briefcase—used in the job he helped me to acquire.

To Gary Yazwa, my undying respect and my interest (separate from Donna's) in
the Lot in Pinetop.

(Continued)

To my friend Jeanne Pepper I leave my bicycle and my best wishes for fertility.

To the Tempe Boys and Girls Club, I leave $500 for the foundation and all my personal effects that Donna does not want to keep.

Most of all, to my wife Donna, I leave all the best of my worldly possessions, interests and rights. Please sell my Earth Systems business to Ernie Carreon if he wants it. To my only true love, the woman who shared the best part of my life, I leave my wish for a long, active, prosperous and fertile life and all the good things that come to her because of her faith and goodness. Please remarry and have the children you so desire.

I name my wife Donna as the executor of my estate. As such I do not wish to burden her with my body, only my memory. The body shall be cremated and scattered in the winds of an Arizona storm.

Dated this day, July 6, 1984

By my hand

Gary Bird

A Manner of Living

If it is true, as it is written in the Bhagavad Gita, that to the illumined man or woman, a clod of dirt, a stone, and gold are the same, then Gary was truly an illumined man. He had no interest in amassing material possessions for himself.

Much of what he "collected" during his life he kept in the night stand next to his side of the bed, the contents of which I stored away in a cardboard box after he died. It contains, among other things, several old pairs of reading glasses, a U.S. Army sewing kit, Jaycees membership card, expired passports, a camouflage make-up kit, address book, University of Arizona license plate, souvenir Fireman's Fund harmonica from the 1999 RIMS conference, a pillowcase printed with the Phelps Dodge mission statement, and dozens of promotional belt buckles, key chains and paperweights.

In addition there was a hunting knife in a leather case, a stack of his old business cards from Phelps Dodge, an unused business card holder much too flashy for his taste, a diver's watch, a dozen or so pocket knives, souvenirs from two Super Bowl games he attended as the guest of a good friend, a visor Amanda made for him in grade school, and a small plastic Yoda (from *Star Wars*) that had been well-chewed by one of the dogs.

In terms of material possessions, this was the fortune Gary left behind. If Gary were ever asked to list all the objects he prized most, his list would probably include: the acre of land he loved to tend, his cowboy boots, saddle, spurs and anything either of the children ever made for him. He also was quite fond of his favorite hand-tooled belt and Western belt buckle.

Yet a list of everything Gary valued most in his life would have nothing material on it. Anyone who ever knew him will tell you the same thing: all that ever mattered to Gary were family, friends, children, animals and service to community. And family would always come first.

Like Gary, I was brought up to honor my family. But as much as Gary was a country boy, I was a city girl, born on the south side of Chicago. And unlike Gary, I was an only child.

My mother, Gertrude Antoinette Lillian Smith, was a single career woman in her mid-thirties working for Johnson & Johnson when she met my father at a ballroom where she and her sister, Charlotte, liked to go dancing twice a week. My mother had great legs to go with her solid, busty figure and dark brown hair that framed her attractive face.

At six feet tall with wavy brown hair, my father was a lot like the priests I knew: congenial and with rosy Irish cheeks. Christened John Joseph Michael Killoughey (did I mention we were Catholic?) my dad served as a radio operator in Okinawa during World War II. Although he had always dreamed of becoming a lawyer, he devoted his entire working life to managing an office at the Social Security Administration. When my mother would say to me, "You're just like your father," I always took it as a compliment. He had a gift for making friends; talking to people came naturally to him.

In contrast, the word "grating" probably best describes my mother's personality. Peace and harmony tended to wither in her presence, so that Dad and I would often seek refuge at a baseball game or at the end of a fishing pole. One of my most vivid childhood memories is of my father and me sitting in a rowboat in the middle of Mud Lake, both pretending not to notice my mother standing on the shore, screaming at us to come in.

At about the age of three, I started spending some nights with my Aunt Charlotte and her family. Charlotte was my mother's sister and possessed a sister's insight and understanding.

"I know your mother loves you, even if she doesn't say so," she would tell me, helping to make up for all those places where my mother was emotionally deficient. Aunt Charlotte provided me with a second home and with cousins—Gloria and Darlene—who became as close as sisters. Two more cousins from my father's side of the family lived just up the street.

Although my mother and I were never close, I can honestly point to her for fostering some of the qualities that have served me best. Along with her love of dancing, I grew to share her industriousness and deep appreciation for the traditions of church and family.

On weekends the whole family gathered at the two-story home of my maternal grandparents; my grandmother and grandfather lived on the second floor while their son occupied the floor below. Every holiday, too, was a family centered event—whether at my grandparents', Charlotte's or our own house.

When I was in second grade my parents and I moved to the suburbs outside of Chicago—to Downers Grove where the train ran through the center of town. When I was young, my mother drove me to school in the mornings, but as a teenager I rode the train to Catholic high school every day. After school—after we rolled up the waistbands of our skirts until the hems were above our knees—my female classmates and I rode the train back home.

After graduation, my mother insisted I commute to college. I chose to attend De Paul University over Loyola, in part, because De Paul was located closest to Union Station in Chicago.

Although I wanted to major in business, the accepted way of thinking among my high school counselors was that girls either became teachers or nurses. So I earned my bachelor's degree in secondary education with the emphasis on math.

From there, life led me to a brief engagement to a college sweetheart, a teaching job in Denver, Colorado, a graduate program in special education at Arizona State University in Phoenix, acceptance into ASU's school of law, my law degree... and Gary.

In Gary I found a kindred spirit. Here was a man who shared my love of family (he introduced me to his entire family at his grandparents' house), my yen for adventure (he was a cowboy who was willing to learn scuba diving and skiing just to date me), and even my keen sense of organization.

Besides all that, Gary was just an all-around good guy.

As the cards and letters poured in after he died, I underlined with a yellow high lighter every special memory of Gary, every reference to his character. It came as no surprise to me that the words used to describe him were repeated in card after card, letter after letter.

A kind and caring person...
Kind heart and selfless acts of giving...
Friendly and kind...
Unassuming, kind ways...
Dedication and professionalism, friendship and caring...
Kind, gentle and unfailingly patient...
Always a gentleman...
A great listener...
Ability to listen and respond...
Character and integrity...

*Always ready to pitch in and give his best, above and beyond
what the average person would do...
A quiet person who got things done...
Supportive and comforting...
A true humanitarian...
He had a gift for helping others...
Someone who does his job, takes care of his family
and does not feel the need to tell everyone how great he is doing at both.*

One woman who only saw Gary's photograph on a website honoring victims of 9/11 posted this message:

I read the portraits every day. This one really touched me, especially the photograph—his face was the essence of kindness.

Whether evidence of the way God works or just ironic, Gary never sought glory in his work and yet it came to him anyway. Gary's only missions in life were to care for his family and his animals, create an environment of safety for men working in harm's way and provide the children in his community with opportunities to grow up happy and successful. Yet an international award is presented annually in his name. He would find that humbling. There was never ego, only pride, in everything he did. He had a passion for doing whatever he could to better someone else's life.

At Gary's memorial celebration, his brother Tom stood at the lectern, his suit and tie disguising his true cowboy spirit. Tom, a university professor, took care to make eye contact with everyone seated throughout the church as, with measured words, he captured the essence of a man whose greatness came—as he saw it—from a simple manner of living:

It seems to me that the manner of Gary's dying was something like lightning; it had nothing to do with his manner of living and it is the manner of his living that we are here to remember and celebrate today.

We are living in the midst of dramatic events—heroes' funerals on television. And so it might not seem like much to say that Gary was a decent, generous and practical man. But decent, generous and practical describe very well his manner of living—with his family and his community and his work.

I suppose each of us connects with Gary's manner of living in different ways. I always liked to hear him talk about his work in risk management. He gave a good deal of himself to that. I can hear the impatience in his voice when he talked about large organizations that would just buy insurance and wait for it to pay off when people were hurt or killed. For Gary the decent and practical thing to do was to also press a safety program so that fewer people were hurt or killed in the first place. He was fortunate that he was able to do that work in a large organization where he served many people; they were fortunate that he was there doing it.

I went searching for words of weight and meaning to express Gary's manner of living. In the end, I found that his manner of living is what gives weight and meaning to the words. And so it seems to me that to call Gary a decent, generous and practical man is to say a great deal indeed.

Family Album

At fifteen I became inspired to join the Junior National Ski Patrol by one of my teachers who spent her weekends patrolling a popular nearby ski hill. To get hired on, she told me, I'd have to successfully complete Red Cross training in first aid, so I immediately enrolled in a class. Once I had my certificate in hand, I showed up at the ski hill where the guy in charge told me I could start immediately—an offer I found surprising considering I didn't know how to ski. No one had mentioned a word to me about that. Whether because I was cute or because they had a lot of free time on their hands, the instructors and ski patrol members there at the hill taught me to ski. The sport became a passion and my years with the ski patrol ignited what was to become a lifelong dedication to service.

Gary and I had dated about six months when I took him to see a film by Warren Miller, director of dozens of movies about skiing. I remember watching Gary, who had been on skis just once or twice in his life, studying the movie with the intensity of a law student preparing to take the Bar. By the time the credits rolled, Gary figured he had a pretty good grasp of the basic moves involved, and he agreed to join me on a four-day ski trip to Durango, CO, with the Phoenix Ski Club.

Sometime into the second day, Gary got so frustrated, he bent one of his ski poles in half. "Looks like now you're going to have to learn to ski with one pole," I told him. (People have learned never to look to a member of our family for a whole lot of sympathy, especially for something they brought on themselves.)

By the end of Day Three, Gary had taught himself to ski through sheer, unbridled determination. He became an excellent skier, one whose passion for a downhill run on six inches of fresh powder matched my own.

He would never have settled for anything less.

Home Movies

We're at Sea World in San Diego. I'm looking through the camera lens at Gary, Amanda and Andrew standing among the crowd gathered at the edge of a pool to feed the dolphins. Amanda and Andrew lean out over the water, waiting for a chance to touch one of the creatures as it swims up to take a fish from a spectator's hand.

As a dolphin approaches, Amanda misses her chance to make contact with it, pulling her hand away at the critical moment. Meanwhile Andrew extends his arm as far as it will stretch and his fingers brush against the mammal's skin. Amanda complains to Gary about the unfairness of Andrew getting to feel the dolphin when she didn't.

"You have to reach out," Gary tells her. "It isn't going to come to you."

You Have to Reach

Gary always made lists—lots and lots of lists. So did I, but while my lists dealt primarily with day-to-day tasks, Gary's outlined in broad strokes the goals he set for his entire life. I got my first look at one of those lists six months after we met, after he asked me to marry him. Right there in bold letters were the words, "Get married by June."

Check.

Back then I didn't give much thought to planning out my future. I was still the girl who had based her choice of colleges mostly on its proximity to the train station.

When I met Gary in June of 1981, I was in the process of becoming a certified scuba diver—a sport I chose based entirely on the kind of men I thought likely to engage in it. Scuba diving required brains, physical fitness, a spirit of adventure, willingness to travel and a job that supplied the means to cover the expense—not coincidentally many of the qualities I was looking for in a partner. I was looking forward to a September trip to Cozumel where I hoped to enjoy some extraordinary diving and meet a great guy in the same week.

I met Gary at a backyard party that a friend pressured me to go to, when all I wanted to do that evening was to curl up on my couch with my dog. Actually I was in the process of leaving the party when Gary hurried over to introduce himself and initiated a conversation that lasted for several hours. At some point I told him about learning to dive and about my plans for Cozumel. The next thing I knew, Gary had not only signed up to take scuba classes, he'd signed up for the same trip.

Darn, I thought. *There goes my chance to meet somebody.*

I had no idea my scuba diving excursion fit so well with Gary's master plan for his life or, for that matter, God's master plan for me.

I can only imagine the supreme effort Gary had to have made to learn to scuba dive in the few short weeks leading up to the trip. I later witnessed that same raw determination in him both in learning to ski and to navigate a wakeboard. Once Gary made up his mind to do something, he would not stop until he succeeded.

Gary always brought that same resolute spirit to everything he did. The 1968 Mohave County Union High School yearbook lists Gary's activities and honors during his high school career (the numbers 1 through 4 denoting the class years in which they occurred): Student Council 4; Junior Play 3; Senior Play 4; Letterman's Club 4; Football 3, 4; Honorable Mention All Conference Tackle; National Honor Society 3, 4; Senior Class President; Student Rotarian for November, 4; Science Club 3; Olathe H.S. Football 1, 2; Basketball 1, 2; Class President 1; Student Council 1, 2.

This is how the parking lot behind the new building looks at 7:30 a.m. on a school day. There is quite a difference at 8:30 a.m. when it is crowded with cars belonging to students and teachers.

(These photos are from Gary's 1968 high school yearbook, illustrating how different the school parking lot looks between the hours of 7:30 and 8:30 in the morning. Guess whose Volkswagen is the first car there?)

Gary's goal-oriented nature seemed programmed into his DNA.

On the Myers-Briggs personality test, Gary scored as an INTJ, interpreted as "Introverted Intuition Thinking Judging." As described on his test results report:

> *INTJ people are relentless innovators in thought as well as action. They trust their own intuitive insights as to the true relationships and meanings of things, regardless of established authority or popularly accepted beliefs. Their faith in their inner vision of new possibilities is so great that they can move mountains. Problems only stimulate them—the impossible takes a little longer, but not much.*
>
> *Being sure of the worth of their inspirations, INTJ people want to see them worked out in practice, applied and accepted by the rest of the world and spend any time and effort necessary to that end. They use their thinking to organize the steps to be taken and overcome opposition. They have determination, perseverance and enduring purpose and drive others almost as hard as they drive themselves...*

Gary's colleagues will attest that this analysis was right on the money. Anyone who ever worked with him will tell you Gary had a distinct philosophy and personality when it came to business. In business, as in all things, he believed you have to reach for what you want.

After earning his degree in business administration from the University of Arizona, Gary devoted his entire professional life to the field of insurance and risk management, his focus kept firmly on the safety of people working in hazardous conditions and on the well-being of their families. Gary began his career as the underwriting supervisor for a company specializing in personal property and casualty insurance. For the next decade he worked for the Salt River Project (SRP) in the area of risk management where he was the first to implement safety practices for construction workers at one of the company's Arizona power plants. Gary believed in protecting the safety of the company's greatest assets—the construction workers in the field—despite the high cost of employing full-time safety experts on remote sites. Despite the doubters' dire predictions, Gary's visionary approach of "safety first" not only saved the company more than $1 million that would otherwise have been paid out in workers' compensation and general liability, it greatly decreased the number of accidents among the company's greatest assets: the construction workers in the field. Gary's approach proved to be a win-win proposition for everyone.

While employed at SRP, Gary rose to the position of vice president of the Arizona Chapter of Risk and Insurance Management Society, Inc. (RIMS) He later became president.

He then went on to serve as director of risk management for Phelps Dodge Corporation, a multinational mining and manufacturing firm headquartered in Phoenix.

Ric Glover—Gary's colleague at Phelps Dodge and sometimes trail ride companion—recalls that when Gary joined the company the mines operated by Phelps Dodge were considered to be the safest in the world, with an average of one contractor killed every eighteen months. Ric told me Gary found it inconceivable that any company accepted a single death without working to do something about it.

So Gary came up with a partnership approach in which the company would provide insurance and implement safety programs for contractors who, in turn, would deduct a percentage of the construction bid. Over the next ten years, not only did the company's mining operations suffer no fatalities, but Gary also saw to it that contractors were reimbursed funds when he discovered the deductions from their bids were too high for the level of risk involved.

While I was quite familiar with the running lists Gary kept at home, Ric remembers the list Gary kept in the right hand desk drawer in his office—the list of what he wanted to accomplish on the job. Ric worked with Gary for five full years designing an insurance program, negotiating with underwriters whose job it was to look for everything that could possibly go wrong in a mining operation. Rock slides, soil migration—the list went on and on.

At last the day came when all the parties involved were satisfied, the papers all signed and stamped.

Ric remembers that the first thing Gary did was open his desk drawer, pull out his list and say, "Okay, what's next?"

Ric says he looked at him and said, "Can't we take just ten minutes to enjoy this?"

Gary wrote what is still considered the authoritative book in his field: *The Wrap-Up Guide,* a manual on how to implement and administer successful controlled insurance programs. Published by the International Risk Management Institute, Inc. (IRMI), Gary wrote the first three editions of the book, currently in its fourth edition thanks to insurance professionals, including Ric, who continue to expand on Gary's vision.

When he was alive, Gary was considered the leading expert in insurance consolidation and risk management for large construction projects. So much so that a colleague Gary worked with in New Mexico posted this message on the Internet after his death:

> *It is highly ironic that his life was snuffed out in one of the worst workers'compensation disasters in the history of the nation.*

Another colleague sent me this letter:

> *I am spending the bulk of my days lately coordinating the insurance portion of a walk-in legal clinic that is providing pro bono assistance to World Trade Center victims (small businesses and individuals). The Association of the Bar of the City of New York is sponsoring the effort, which also provides real estate, tax and other advice to victims...*
>
> *One of my first tasks was to put together a list of the types of policies that could be triggered by recent events—and my first thought was to run the draft list past Gary to see what I had forgotten. He was always my expert, making sure I didn't get sloppy or careless. I wish he could be here helping now.*

Both literally and figuratively, Gary always wanted to keep his sights fixed on the horizon, to continually reach beyond his grasp, no matter how distant the destination or how long it took to get there. In his memory, IRMI changed the name of its annual best practices award for innovation in the field of construction risk management to *The Gary E. Bird Horizon Award*. Those of us who knew him can tell you such recognition would make him uncomfortable. He was quick to give the credit to others and he found as much or more satisfaction in helping others reach for their horizons than he did in arriving at his own.

Here's a perfect illustration.

Once when our family was going on vacation, a good friend of ours, Karen Salem, asked to take care of the horses while we were away. Though she had never had a horse of her own, she'd always dreamed that one day she would. So before we left, she came over to have Gary instruct her on all the do's and don'ts she needed to know in caring for the horses every day, twice a day.

By the time we returned home, she admitted to feeling both inspired and exhausted by her crash course in horses.

She was about to leave when Gary asked her to wait a minute, that he had something he wanted to give her. He came back and handed her one of the metal hitches used to tow a horse trailer.

"You'll have your horse someday," he told her. "Here's something to get you started."

The fastest way to train a horse is to take your time doing it.
            – Rocco Wachman, from *Cowboy*

Gary always reached for whatever he wanted and he encouraged our children to do the same. "Our children" included Matthew Angleman. Gary and Matt's father, Chris, had been roommates when the two attended the University of Arizona. Soon after Gary and I moved with nearly two-year-old Amanda into a new home in a quiet Tempe neighborhood, Gary was shocked one day to look across the fence and discover that his former roommate had just moved into the house next door with his wife and two-year-old Matt.

Matt became an extension of our growing family, even joining us on many of our family vacations to Colorado. Matt vividly remembers one particular trip when he was about twelve, when Gary took him out on the slopes for his first private lesson in snowboarding—an experience Matt describes as "nerve wracking" as he witnessed the funny, carefree father of his two best friends (a man he thought of as a "second father") transform into an instructor with a stern, no-nonsense, show-no-mercy teaching style.

"Gary had a strong presence, very tough love," he recalls. Matt says that the fact he was the timid sort who feared falling down and getting hurt garnered no sympathy from Gary.

Words for Gary

Words cannot
Fathom
Changes in life
Brought down upon my growing soul
All of us

Without warning
Stolen from

Still I
See you in everything
What makes a watchful eye appear
At a glance
Teacher

For what is not there
Beckons
Lays in wait
A dove
Staring into my passion
A life so beautiful

Understanding loss
Impossible cause

So instead
I pray for
Him:

Animal Dreamer
spirit by our side
Love is infinite and so shall these scars
on our palms help us
Heal
Remember
September

(Written by Matt Angleman, then 15, soon after Gary's death)

"He would yell at me to *Get back up! Don't quit!"*

There were years, Matt says, when he thought about not coming with us to Colorado, knowing that if he did, he would be facing another session with Gary.

"But it all paid off, I guess, because I'm really good at snowboarding now."

Gary always did more than simply ask his children to try their best, he actively supported their efforts. In grade school when Andrew wanted to play basketball and Pop Warner football, Gary took him to practice after school and attended every game.

Andrew also remembers the year's worth of Saturdays he and his father took piano lessons together. Learning to play the piano was Gary's idea. Andrew wanted to play the drums. Gary agreed to let Andrew take drum lessons, but only after he had spent a year building a musical foundation on the piano.

Although more than ten years have passed, Andrew vividly remembers the stern old woman who came to our home to teach him and his dad.

"She always had a music book in her hand and whenever one of us missed a note, she slapped us with it. Dad was always laughing about it."

Andrew stuck it out. True to his word, Gary let him quit after the year was up. Gary died not long afterwards.

Andrew did get to take his drum lessons. Marsh USA sent both of our children some money with instructions for each of them to buy something they really wanted. Andrew chose a drum set and he continues to play the drums to this day.

After Gary was invited by Tempe's mayor to sit on the city's Industrial Development Authority Board, he voluntarily took on the additional role as head of the board's scholarship committee. He worked with all five area high schools, encouraging students to apply. Fellow committee member John "Hut" Hutson remembers the time each year when the committee interviewed up to forty applicants in a single day. The only requirements were that the student neither be in the bottom fifty percent nor the top five percent of their class in grade point average, because other funding was available to kids who fell into those categories. Students awarded the scholarships could apply them wherever they wanted, to a university or a trade school. What mattered to Gary, Hut remembers, is that kids went on to be productive, contributing members of the community. He wanted them to experience the same pride and satisfaction in accomplishment that he felt in setting a goal and going after it.

Who knows why and how circumstances manage to align in a way that places someone we love in harm's way? And when they do, when a loved one is taken from us suddenly, unexpectedly and with so many dreams left to reach for, it can be tempting to get caught in the trap of "if only."

Gary's colleague and close friend Mike Goss personally knew sixty of the people who died on 9/11. Of all of them, Gary's loss was the hardest for Mike, in part because he was closest to Gary, but also because he was the one who convinced the powers that be at Marsh to hire Gary for the position that sent him to New York City that day.

Mike still cries when he speaks of it.

"There's no way he would have been sitting on the 99th floor if I hadn't pushed the way I did."

If only...

And yet just four months earlier, Mike was successful in getting another young Marsh employee named Brian transferred from the New York offices to Phoenix. If Mike hadn't pushed on Brian's behalf, in all probability Brian would have been in the World Trade Center towers that morning, leaving his wife and two young children to mourn his loss.

If only...

In the process of creating this book, while going through boxes of old papers, I came across Gary's flight itinerary for the conference in Denver where he was originally scheduled to be on 9/11. The program was there, too, with Gary's name listed as a featured speaker.

It might be easy to look at those and think, *if only...* But to do that would be to deny the passion and joy with which Gary lived. Gary, of all people, knew life comes with risks. He knew the decision to go to New York had its risks, but he chose to go anyway. He went happily, filled with the excitement of taking on a new challenge and striving to reach new goals.

Andrew and Amanda both will tell you that if their father's death has taught them anything, it is the importance of living every day to the fullest. They'll say that lesson comes, not from lamenting anything their father left undone, but from recognizing how much he was able to accomplish in the time he was alive. They'll tell you he never took a break from fully engaging in his family, his friends, his work and his interests—in horses, skiing, sailing...even piano. A scholarship fund created in his memory continues to support young people who not only serve their communities, but do so with the same faith-filled spirit Gary brought to everything he did.

Gary's life is a testament to his belief that if you want to enjoy everything the world has to offer, you have to reach. I have always shared that belief, although there were moments following his death when I had to reflect on just what I should reach for.

Before 9/11, I based my actions—on everything from my law practice, to caring for aging parents, to where to go on vacation—on my answers to three questions:

What does God want me to do?

What decision or action enhances my relationship with Gary?

What decision best serves the welfare of our children?

The answers I received through prayerful reflection made my choices, if not always easy, at least clear.

In the first days following 9/11, I was certain of only one thing: I did not want my children to become orphans. I resolved to do everything within my power to stay healthy, and to be strong and present for Amanda and Andrew. I rearranged my life to make that happen, which meant stepping back from my law practice and spending the majority of my time at home.

The transition from wife to widow led me to question my identity: *Who am I apart from Gary? Apart from the life we created together?*

I asked God *every day* what to do. And every day I felt the same guidance: *Do very little. "Be" with your feelings of grief, pain and uncertainty. Allow others to assist you and care for you. Don't make any big changes.*

I felt invited to fully experience the love and care being offered to me by friends, family, even strangers. I felt invited to fully embrace the blessings that are my children. I felt invited to take the time to rest without having to reach for anything.

From that point on, I began to experience my life as a series of invitations. I eventually returned to my law practice focused more than ever on bringing peace to situations involving conflict, especially matters of probate or administering trust estates after death. Then in 2004, Father Dale approached me and posed this question: *Are you ready to make a transition?*

The transition he proposed was to go to work in the area of development for *Life Teen,* an organization he founded at St. Timothy's in 1985 with the purpose of leading teens closer to Christ.

That simple invitation again led to me question my identity: *Who am I apart from the law, from my work as an attorney?*

Yet when I asked myself if I was ready to make a transition, I knew in my heart the answer was "Yes."

A little more than eighteen months later, another invitation led to a six-month sabbatical that began with a three-week tour of Europe with Gary's stepmother. On our way home, we came through New York on September 8. Three days later I was in Phoenix attending the dedication for the 9/11 Memorial outside the Arizona State Capitol Building.

I woke up the next day with a clean slate—with no e-mail address, no fax number and nothing penciled on the calender. I cleared my life of all distractions and focused only on those activities that served my spiritual, physical, intellectual and emotional needs.

The day came when I felt God tapping on my shoulder again, calling me to something new. My phone rang and a friend at the other end of the line asked, "Are you bored yet? Want to come work at St. Vincent de Paul and help with grant writing?"

Today I am in charge of donor relations for the Society of St. Vincent de Paul Phoenix. It is my joy and privilege to serve as a steward for people who give generously in support of the poor. Here in Phoenix we have 15,000 active donors. It is my job to create and implement a program that ensures they feel valued, not only for their monetary gifts, but also for the gifts they are as members of our community. For me, the task of making every one of them feel acknowledged and appreciated is not just a goal worth reaching for; it is an invitation I feel blessed to accept.

Amanda and Andrew

Family Album

I am reminded of a line from Grantland Rice's poem *Casey's Revenge* about a baseball player: *Fame is fleeting as the wind and glory fades away.*

Minutes after our plane landed under a tropical sky, Gary and I stepped down the passenger stairs at the Goldson International Airport in Belize to begin a week of sightseeing, scuba diving and deep sea fishing. Just inside the terminal entrance, our plane load of passengers was met by a group of about twenty airport employees dressed in white uniforms, all talking excitedly and straining to see over each other's shoulders.

Curious, Gary and I stopped to ask what all the fuss was about and were told that word had leaked out that a celebrity was aboard our plane. And not just any celebrity, but one especially revered by the people of this basketball fanatical country— twelve-time NBA All-Star...

Larry Bird.

Fame was never more fleeting than it was for the employees of the Belize airport that day. For us, however, the memory of that mix-up never ceased to make us laugh.

Family Album

He feels like Dad and sounds like Dad...

When our children were small, Halloween was a huge event in the Tempe neighborhood where we lived. In late afternoon when it was still light outside, all the children would dress up in their costumes and parade through the streets to the local park where the parents put on a party with drinks and snacks.

Later in the evening when the trick-or-treating got underway, I took Amanda and Andrew from house to house, while Gary sat in a lawn chair on our driveway doing his best Yoda impression and passing out candy to the children.

I May Be Stupid, But I'm Ugly!

That was one of Gary's favorite lines. *I may be stupid, but I'm ugly!*

Gary was a man who took his commitments and responsibilities—to his family, his friends and his profession—very seriously. But he was also someone who loved to laugh, especially at himself.

On my birthday one year he gave me a card with a cartoon figure of a man underneath the words: *To my wife. It's your birthday, Honey, and I just want to remind you that, no matter what, you'll always have me!*

On the inside, it read, *And if you can overcome that you can overcome anything!*

Among his circle of family and friends—particularly among the children—Gary became famous for his uncannily realistic, and decidedly undignified, chicken impression. It often began unexpectedly, with just a subtle change in his expression. Then his neck began to move, forwards and back, forwards and back, swiveling left and then right as his chin pecked at the air and his hands tucked under his armpits. By the time he added the legs—strutting in jerky, uneven movements across the floor—he had everyone aching with laughter.

After Gary died, I asked Gary's friends and colleagues to send me their favorite memories of him. His sense of humor was the topic of so many stories I received, including this one from a colleague at Phelps Dodge:

Along about 1997, Gary and I were in Silver City, New Mexico, to conduct a seminar for the folks at the Chino and Tyrone mining operations. Over breakfast the morning of the seminar, Gary outlined the message he planned to deliver that day on the subject of safety. He said he would implore each one of us to be especially diligent in our own actions so as to prevent accidents. As a corporate risk manager, this was a hot button issue for Gary and on that morning his pump was primed on the subject.

As I started my car for the drive out to the mine, Gary sat next to me in the passenger seat, still expounding on the topic of safety. I threw the car into reverse, stepped on the gas pedal and slammed into the car parked behind us.

Gary turned to me and said, "Weren't you listening to me at all?"

As was the custom at all our meetings at the mine, another colleague put out a request for a "safety share"—an invitation to relate any new developments on the subject.

Gary looked at me and smiled. "Bob," he said, "I believe this is your time on stage."

In early 2000, Gary traveled to the little copper mining town of Bagdad, Arizona, with two female colleagues from New York. Following their first day's business, the three ate dinner at a restaurant where nearly all the tables remained empty throughout the evening—an unsettling sight for two women accustomed to crowded, big city dining rooms. The 2000 census listed the population of Bagdad as 1,578.

After dinner his colleagues drove Gary through Bagdad's dimly lit streets to the single townhouse unit the company had reserved for him. Before going on to the house the two women were to share, they waited inside the car, training the headlights on Gary until they could see he was safely inside the building.

They watched him enter, only to see him come flying out the door and fall backwards onto the sidewalk. Too stunned to know how to react, the women saw Gary jump to his feet, roll up his sleeves and march back into the building, fists up as though gearing up for a fight. A few seconds later Gary reappeared at the door, triumphant, dusting off his hands and looking like Chuck Norris after fending off three thugs in an alley.

Then with a smile and a wave, Gary left his once anxious colleagues laughing as they drove away.

The laughter Gary brought to my life is a light that never goes out. I'll always remember the NBA game Gary took me to for Valentines Day one year. He got great seats for us to cheer on the Phoenix Suns. I don't recall who we were playing that night, but I do remember seeing the Suns mascot, the hairy T-shirt clad Gorilla, come charging up the steps toward us, passing right beside me before delivering an orange and purple warm-up suit to a woman two rows up—the same orange and purple warm-up suit Gary had made careful arrangements to be delivered to *me*.

Yet thanks to that little mistake, a delighted woman got a free warm-up suit for no reason at all, I got a special visit from the Suns Gorilla in my office a few weeks later—where I got a replacement suit and a mascot plush toy signed by the Gorilla himself—and Gary and I got a whole lot of laughs.

Thanks to Gary, I have so many memories that can make me laugh to this day. Sometime after he died, I went on a rafting trip through the Grand Canyon with my cousin Gloria. As we drifted along a calm place in the river, Gloria and I were positioned at the front of the raft—a spot our guide referred to as the "bird bath" because that's where the most water splashes in. We weren't talking, just taking in the awe-inspiring views of canyon walls, when Gloria tapped my forearm to get my attention.

I looked over to see a Great Blue Heron flying alongside our raft. It kept pace with us for what seemed a mile or more, as though attached to the end of a kite string. Then as we approached a stretch of open beach, it flew on ahead and glided gracefully onto the sand where it finally came to rest, folding its great wings.

I sat transfixed by the grace and beauty of one of God's creatures...for about five seconds. Then all of a sudden the heron's head began a slow, rhythmic motion back and forth, pecking at the air with its long beak as its legs strutted in slow, jerky movements across the sand.

In one of those rare, sublime moments when tears and laughter come together, Gloria and I both agreed we were blessed for the opportunity to see Gary do his chicken dance, one more time.

Family Album

Gary and I both travelled a lot for our careers. My service to the American Bar Association required that I travel to conferences four times a year for four to five days at a time to work with fellow attorneys on how to improve their law practices. Once when Amanda was three, Gary took her to visit a family friend who asked Amanda where her mommy was.

"Oh, that Donna!" Amanda answered, mimicking my mother. "She's gone again on another trip."

More than one colleague asked me, "How can you go off and leave your husband with your kids?"

The question never ceased to amaze me. Seriously, what woman in her right mind would choose a husband she didn't trust with her kids? I started wondering whether it was to sheer luck that I owed the good fortune of having a husband as responsible and nurturing to our children as I was.

Whether I was home or away, Gary was a fully involved, change the diaper, read the bedtime story, bake the birthday cake, get down on the floor and play with blocks kind of parent from day one. I was away on another ABA trip when this photo was taken. Before I left, I encouraged Gary to take Amanda to the annual Halloween party sponsored by a local businessman. "Oh, and by the way," I told him, "I haven't had time to put together any costumes."

The party, the costumes, the short notice—none of it posed any problem for Gary. With the same gusto he approached everything else in his life, he pieced together the clothing and accessories to transform his daughter into Tinker Bell and himself into Peter Pan, lime green tights and all.

Holiday Greetings from the Birds
1995

We have so many blessings to be thankful for this past year. Perhaps most importantly is that Birds flew the old coop in late July and winged it to another residence in South Tempe, which we now fondly refer to as "The Bird Ranch." (Gary has written this in rather large letters on the mailbox in case you might miss it.) Gary feels as though he has finally "come home again" because "the ranch" is more than an acre with a horse pasture, a view of the sunrise and no fences to obstruct the view of our neighborhood chickens and guinea hens chasing each other across the back half-acre (we don't have a back-forty yet). Gary spent a good part of Halloween weekend building a chicken condo with four units, so now we have more brown eggs than anyone could ever eat. If you want some, just stop by with an empty egg carton.

This is Heaven

One afternoon just before Memorial Day 1995, I got a voice mail message from my cousin Darlene.

"I've just been to a birthday party at a place in Tempe that I think is perfect for Gary," she said. "And it just went on the market."

Darlene went on to describe this property with its horse corrals and stables in an area designed for people who keep large animals. Gary had been looking for just such a place since his father died. Gary had chosen to keep two of his father's horses and while he found a ranch near our home to board them, what he most wanted was a small piece of ranch land to call his own. And the sooner the better.

I resisted the idea of moving. For one thing, I loved our home in suburbia with its vaulted ceilings, open floor plan and generous windows for letting in the light. Over the years we'd created the perfect backyard complete with patio, green grass, shade trees, picnic table, barbecue, sandbox, swing set, kids' clubhouse—and all of it surrounded by neighbors who'd become part of our extended family.

Many of our closest neighbors at this country house, on the other hand, were the chickens and guinea hens that roamed through the yard. The house was a throwback to the 1960s with its dark, low-hanging cabinets in the kitchen, the dingy beige carpeting in the living room and—my personal favorite—the master bathroom's harvest gold bathtub and shower combination installed below the floor level and facing an atrium to the south. Not even the toilet was enclosed to allow for any privacy.

Did my marriage vows require that I exchange an already comfortable and content existence for this? The unbridled enthusiasm written all over Gary's face said "Yes."

We learned early on in our marriage that the only time we could count on was the present.

It was a Friday afternoon just two weeks after our wedding when Gary and I found ourselves in a doctor's exam room as she broke the news that I had malignant skin cancer. I had first called attention to the red spot on my neck when I went to see my OB/GYN for the blood test required for a marriage license. Though she didn't think there was any reason for concern, she recommended I go to a dermatologist as soon as Gary and I returned from our honeymoon. Now this skin doctor was insisting that I not let another minute pass before having this lesion surgically removed. She did not want it to grow over the weekend.

By now Gary's tanned, post-honeymoon complexion had turned the color of skim milk, so my doctor suggested he not stick around for the procedure. So while my doctor worked to remove the growth and enough healthy tissue around it to require twenty-two stitches to close the gap, Gary sat in an increasingly crowded waiting room, wrestling with the possibility of going from newlywed to widower before our first anniversary. We went home to wait for tests results that would tell us whether or not I'd require any additional treatment.

By Monday afternoon we were back to celebrating. While my condition required careful monitoring, with check-ups every three months for the next five years, my prognosis was excellent. But she had one caveat.

"I'd strongly advise against getting pregnant anytime soon," she said, explaining that medical research had not yet ruled out a possible link between the hormones that occur in pregnancy and the development of melanoma.

Counting our many blessings, Gary and I went home intent on celebrating our lives as a couple.

After nearly three years with no signs of cancer, I became pregnant. But our joy was short-lived; I miscarried at seven weeks.

Two months later I was standing at a counter picking up some clothes at the dry cleaner's when I started to feel light headed and weak. I remember very little after that, as I drifted in and out of consciousness on the shopkeeper's floor, in the back of an ambulance and in the hospital emergency room. I woke up after surgery to learn the fallopian tube on my left side had burst from an ectopic pregnancy and that the surgeon had never seen a patient so close to death and yet manage to survive.

For the second time in our young marriage, Gary and I were confronted with life's unpredictable and even precarious nature. All we did know for certain was how precious we were to each other and how committed we were to showing gratitude and respect for everything we had in any given moment. Not every couple is faced with the potential loss of one partner so early on in marriage. For us it proved to be a blessing, one that set the tone for our relationship from that point on.

I don't mean to create the impression that we were perfect—either as individuals or as a couple. When it came to politics, we were polar opposites—the only thing we came to agree on was that we should never, ever discuss politics with each other.

Why throw cold water on all those warm, fuzzy feelings we had learned never to take for granted? So with every election, we each dutifully went to the polls with the full knowledge our votes cancelled each other out and we might just as well have stayed home.

Gary and I had different interests, as well, but we supported each other in going after whatever we most wanted in life.

And for Gary, one of the things he wanted most in his life was a piece of land in the country where he could have horses. Which is how we came to live in that decorator's nightmare of a house with flocks of guinea hens roaming through the yard.

The temperature hit 118 degrees the day we moved in. At some point I lay down spread eagle on the tiled kitchen floor, hoping for one brief, cooling reprieve. But it was nowhere to be found.

One of our first mornings in the house, I stepped into the tile-lined hole in the ground that passed as a shower and felt a searing pain in my right foot. I looked down to discover that the harvest gold tile provided the perfect camouflage for the scorpion that had sought refuge there. I got my mobile phone and called Gary who was driving to the co-op in his air-conditioned truck to get hay and feed for the horses. Despite all his years in Arizona, Gary had never been stung by one of these poisonous creatures and wasn't certain what to advise. Panicked by not knowing what to do when I lost feeling up to my ankle, I dialed the poison control center where the person at the other end of the line told me that, as long as I showed no signs of a serious allergy to scorpion venom—hives, shortness of breath, vomiting—I should take triple doses of Tylenol, elevate my foot and pack it in ice. Crisis averted.

Our nearest human neighbors were Deb and Terry Keller. Deb has had a long career as a publicist for comedians including Paula Poundstone, Dane Cook, Jeff Dunham and Bobcat Goldthwait. Deb and Gary proved to be kindred spirits when it came to the raising of both horses and children. While I spent every Saturday morning running errands and shopping for the week's groceries, Gary stayed behind to watch over the kids and often chatted about horses and child-related matters with Deb over the chain-link fence that divided our properties.

When we went on vacation, Deb took over the care and feeding of our horses, following the exhaustive list of instructions Gary always provided.

So when more help is needed, the rancher calls up his neighbors, who are usually ranchers or ranch managers themselves.
　　　　　　　　　　　　　　　　　　　　　　　　　– Rocco Wachman, from *Cowboy*

Deb and Terry had been long-time residents along our country road well before we came along, and Deb was the established contact for all issues affecting the neighborhood. When the need arose to clear the irrigation ditch that ran along all of our properties, it fell to her to organize a planning meeting.

Deb still remembers her frustration at trying to come up with a meeting date to suit everyone, and she says she's never forgotten what Gary told her when she voiced her frustration to him over the back fence:

"If there's one thing I know, people like to be led," he told her. "You pick the day and they will come. Those to whom it matters will come."

There was a bit of cowboy wisdom in everything Gary did.

If you have to use your rope, you've done something wrong... It's one of those situations where the less pressure a cowboy puts on the cattle, the more receptive the cows will be to following the cowboy's wishes.

– Rocco Wachman, from *Cowboy*

Even back when Gary and I met, I should have been able to predict the country life I'd be living one day. I might have guessed when he took me dove hunting on one of our first dates, or when he took me out to hunt javelina in Arivaca over Thanksgiving—although for as many of the creatures we saw that day, we could just as well have called it "hiking"—or when he gave me my first cowboy hat for my birthday.

But one of the greatest and most precious things about Gary was that he never set out to mould me into anyone other than who I was. Nor did I have any desire to change him. A big part of what made our marriage work was the freedom we gave each other to do, to be and to have all that we most wanted.

Both of our careers involved extensive traveling, sometimes separating us for weeks at a time. One of Gary's trips for Phelps Dodge lasted forty-five days with stops in New York, South Carolina, Bermuda, England, Germany, Thailand, Manila and Singapore. While he was away, I went to my job, cared for the kids and held down our somewhat rickety country fort with its fragile plumbing and never-ending need for repairs.

He did the same for me whenever I traveled, whether for business or just for the adventure. In 2000, the year I turned fifty, I decided what I wanted most was to take a sabbatical from my demanding law practice to take our children on a ten-week European tour. Gary gave me and the kids his wholehearted support.

One year we left the kids with their grandmothers and while I followed up a conference in Beijing with a two-week tour of China, Gary went scuba diving in the Caribbean with friends.

Gary and I were as comfortable apart as we were deeply appreciative of the time spent together—as a couple and as a family.

The morning Gary left to go to New York, I found him at the breakfast table, having just come inside from feeding his horses. He sat gazing out the back window at the corrals where he had spent all summer with his "girls."

All he said was, "This is heaven."

Who could have predicted that Gary's dream life in the country would be so short? I thank God every day for the too-few years he had on our little ranch with his horses. I thank God I didn't take one look at that ramshackle house with the horrific harvest gold bathroom and say, "Forget it. We're not living there."

Oh, I thought it—I admit that. Yet I am so grateful I will never have to live with the regret of denying my husband, my companion and my best friend something he wanted and loved so much. I'm grateful we parted with no feeling of love left unexpressed. I'm grateful we had the kind of marriage where neither one of us had to wait to know heaven.

This was my last letter to him:

Dear Gary:

Three weeks ago this morning you were here with us, enjoying the morning, sitting around this table, reading the paper. As usual, I slept in (til 6:50!) and you joshed me about it— you had already visited Jack and fed "the girls" and taken a walk before I came out from behind my blinders.

Our lives were quite content, yet changing, back then. Seems so long ago... We were each studying up on how to recommit to our marriage as we approached the twenty-year mark, and our individual middle ages.

You went out the door with your marriage enrichment book under your arm. I made a note to read mine further while you were gone.

Before leaving at 11 or so, you stopped at my chair, your little suitcase in tow and wearing the shirt and slacks so carefully selected to be the correct combo of business/casual for NYC.

You said, "I'm a little bit scared about this," not so much to express fear as the wonderful challenge of a new job, new people, new achievements to be reached. I commented lightly that your departure was a bit like going off to kindergarten— book under your arm...

We laughed. We shared your joy. We hugged. We said, "I love you," as we always do...then you left us.

Family Album

Some of my most special moments with Gary occurred when he didn't know I was watching. This is one of those moments.

We were attending a friend's wedding, an employee of the Boys and Girls Club that Gary helped to found. I was busy taking photographs of the bride and groom at the reception when I happened to look over at my husband and daughter.

As a toddler, Amanda's thumb rarely left her mouth. She was extremely attached to it. I don't know exactly what led to this moment, but I like to think that in a moment of loving generosity, Amanda reached up and offered her most precious possession to her daddy. Recognizing the sacrifice, her daddy gave her his thumb so that she wouldn't have to go without.

Love Never Ends

I am a little pencil in the hand of a writing God who is sending a love letter to the world.

— Blessed Mother Teresa

At Gary's memorial celebration, Father Dale said that if we can take any lessons from the events of 9/11, from the loss of Gary and so many others, it is that we can "know that love never ends and the spirit never dies."

Moments with Gary did not end with 9/11. You may choose to believe the stories I'm about to share, or you may not. What I know is that the story of Gary's life would not be complete without them, because without them I might not be able to say with such unshakeable certainty that Gary's spirit goes on.

Our neighbors Deb and Terry Keller both had experiences of Gary communicating with them after his death. While Deb is a naturally intuitive person with a long history of receiving messages from the spiritual realm, Terry is your more stereotypical engineer, a left-brain type who operates from logic, reason and cold, hard facts. Yet within hours of the towers collapsing, Terry felt Gary's presence as undeniably as though Gary had just walked through the door of his office. From someplace deep inside, he heard Gary's voice:

Watch over my family.

Terry would later learn that, miles away at precisely the same hour, Deb had felt the same presence and heard the same message.

Months later Deb gave me a piece of paper upon which she had scrawled several messages from Gary—one for each of our children and one for me:

Donna: Must go on with her life. Has done a fantastic job. Take the time to love the children. They need you more than ever—you have the means to make them first before God and the church. They are God.

Amanda: My sweet little pumpkin, you are a beautiful young woman and one of the most precious things in my life. I admire your strength. Take care of yourself and your mother and know I will be there to kiss you every morning.

Andrew: Focus. Focus. Focus. Always remember what you know is right. Be the wise responsible man that I know you are. Don't hide your heart for it is how I will always communicate with you. Take care of your mom and sister.

I will always be with you and love you deeply.

On the evening of September 11, Maureen Adams, a fellow parishioner of St. Timothy's, stopped by our house to check on me and the children. She said she had just attended the evening prayer service where someone had recited a passage from the Bible she thought might be particularly helpful to me. I found the copy of the brand new Bible that Andrew had taken with him to church camp earlier in the summer. I turned to the chapter she cited to find the passages already underlined in ink.

They were the same passages my doctor "prescribed" for me the very next morning: the passages from Romans Chapter 8:38–a chapter that Andrew hadn't studied at camp.

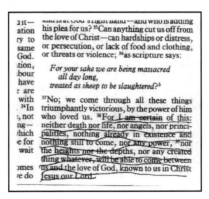

Maureen waited nearly two weeks before sharing another experience she had the evening of 9/11. She, like so many others, wanted to support me in hoping for Gary's safe return for as long as that hope stayed alive.

After hearing Gary may have been near the World Trade Center at the time of the attacks early that morning, Maureen went to the chapel to pray before going on to the evening prayer service in the church. There in the silence, her thoughts turned to the question so many of us who knew and loved him were asking:

"Jesus, where is my friend Gary?"

She repeated the question several times and, receiving no answer, moved on to the church where she took a seat near the back. When she looked up at the altar, she saw an image of Gary dressed in jeans and a red shirt, his right thumb hooked in the side pocket, and smiling in his customarily easy way. Next to Gary, Maureen saw an image of Jesus, his armed wrapped around Gary's shoulders.

It was staggering to hear her describe in detail the shirt Gary was wearing. She knew Gary from church and Gary always dressed up for church. She had no way of knowing the shirt she "saw" in the church that night was Gary's favorite and still hanging in our closet—not until I pulled it out for her to see.

Maureen's experience brought me great comfort. Gary had never suffered beneath a mountain of steel and concrete. He was safe. He was loved. He was smiling.

Sally Putnam is a Harvard educated financial planner I met through our respective service in ministries at St. Timothy's. At the time I was considering starting an Internet based repository for estate planning documents and asked Sally for her expertise as a consultant. Gary sat in on our first planning session, but after that, the only time his path ever crossed with Sally's was at the occasional church function. Once I finally determined that my Internet business was too costly to develop, I saw less of Sally too.

So when she came to me after 9/11 and said she had "seen" Gary during Mass—in the quiet, prayerful moments after Communion—I believed her and for two reasons: professionally I knew Sally to be honest and straightforward and, at the same time, our personal connection was nowhere deep enough for her to know what I might need or want to hear.

As though a memory, Sally said she saw Gary guiding a middle-aged woman from behind her desk in the middle of a large office. While the woman appeared frightened, even frantic, Gary showed no panic, only a sense of urgency as he showed her to a door leading to a stairwell. As he opened the door, his eyes and mouth widened with delight and he said, "Oh, hello, God! I didn't know you were here!"

Sally said that even though she wanted to tell me about her experience the day it happened, the Sunday after the attacks, she chose not to. On that day, she explained, I was still hoping Gary might be found alive, still hoping for a miracle. So she waited until the passage of time had done what she could never bring herself to do: take that hope away.

My cousin Gloria's son Brian, who had developed some skills in video editing, volunteered to put together a film memorial of Gary to show before his memorial Mass. Like other young people his age have been known to do, he procrastinated until the night before the service. He stayed up all night piecing together a series of photographs and setting them to Enya's recording of *Only Time*. With no time left to spare, he went to transfer the entire film from his computer to the videotape he was charged with delivering to the church that morning. That's when he discovered he didn't have the right cord to connect his computer to the VCR. To connect the units, he needed one chord with a "male" connector and one with its "female" counterpart. All he had were a pair of males. In panic and desperation, he brought two "male" ends together, crossing one over the other as though they were two tiny swords, and prayed for a miracle.

He got one. While he stood there for several minutes holding two cords that had no earthly or scientific reason for making a connection, the film tribute of Gary's life and the events of 9/11 travelled from the computer to the videotape just in time.

My friend Donna Alizio told me of a dream she had on three consecutive nights.

In her dream Gary is in a fiery stairwell crowded with people. After reaching through the fire to pull some people through, he makes his way down a flight of stairs toward a frightened woman standing on the landing below.

"I'm scared," she says and Gary encourages her to come with him.

Ric Glover, too, saw Gary in a recurring dream. After Gary's death, Ric started having the same dream, a couple of times a week for several months. Among his wife and every business associate who ever had to share a room with him, Ric had the reputation as someone who could sleep through anything. His wife even had to rouse him from a sound sleep the night a drunken neighbor mistook their house for his own and bashed in the back door. Yet this dream never failed to jerk him awake.

It is the same every time. Gary is standing a ways off, shrouded in mist. Or is it dust? He has that familiar twinkle in his eye as he says, "Partner, you ought not go that way." He flashes a knowing grin. "It's okay," he adds reassuringly. "I know the man at the gate." Just then the haze around him clears enough to reveal a path rising in the distance behind him. Then it's over.

After thirty or more times having his sleep interrupted, Ric was baffled. More than that, he was exhausted.

One morning Ric mentioned to his wife that he'd had "the dream" again and asked for her thoughts on what it might possibly be trying to tell him. From the first night the images appeared to him, he was convinced Gary's presence at the World Trade Center on that September day was by design, for the purpose of liberating another soul. But if that was the message, Ric said to his wife, why did the dream keep recurring?

"Because the message isn't meant for you," she said. "It's for Donna."

Interestingly, after he shared the dream with me, he never had it again. Ric's dream brought me tremendous comfort. It cast yet another light on the goodness present amid all the pain and grief—my own as well as the pain and grief felt by my children, by the families and friends of every person killed on 9/11, by our nation and by an entire community of nations.

The attacks on 9/11 left my cousin Noel stranded in Las Vegas. Rather than rent a car to drive home to Illinois, she came to Phoenix to stay with me and the children through the weekend while we waited for any news about Gary.

She was able to get a flight on Monday the 17th and the following day returned to her office on the 29th floor of a high rise in downtown Chicago. The president of the company was sitting in my cousin's office when a bird landed on the ledge outside the window. About the size of a crow, the bird had a black head and a white breast barred with thin brown bands. The bird peered in through the window as though it had come to sit in on their meeting. Its presence was so unusual, the president started calling in other people to take a look. Finally a coworker who knew something about birds identified the unlikely visitor as a Peregrine Falcon.

When Noel told me about the bird's strange appearance, I knew it was just another of God's signs. Gary loved the trio of ski runs in Beaver Creek, Colorado, known as the "Birds of Prey." They were the most challenging and therefore the runs Gary was most determined to tackle, even though he had fewer than ten days of skiing under his belt. He managed to conquer all three: the Goshawk, the Golden Eagle and the Peregrine.

In 2009 my friend Donna Alizio's husband Tony fell ill on September 11. He died just weeks later.

Donna struggled for months to embrace anything beyond her grief. The Sunday I encountered her at church was the first time she had come to worship in six months.

"I'm stuck," she said to me. She said she couldn't seem to get past the questioning, the anger and the grief.

I did my best in that moment to tell her what I want everyone facing the pain of loss to know: *In my experience, the greatest comfort came from letting it all go and turning it all over to God.*

The following December, Donna called to tell me Tony had appeared to her in a dream with a message Gary wanted her to give me. Gary's message to Tony was that he had wanted to call me from the World Trade Center after the first plane hit, but there wasn't enough time. There were too many people who needed help getting out of the building and he needed to use his training in doing everything he could for them. By the time he reached into his pocket for his cell phone, every ounce of strength was gone.

Tony said that Gary wanted me to know that he loves me and that he had done all the work God meant for him to do on earth. He also wanted me to know that he was "doing great," that he was able to ski as much as he wanted and that I should take a trip to the Galapagos Islands, because he's there in the summer.

In Donna's dream Tony said Gary wanted everyone to know "the real story of 9/11."

Amanda and Andrew have always felt their father's continued presence in their lives. Andrew remembers a particular football game in high school. Andrew was a sophomore playing on the junior varsity squad and this match-up against a rival school happened to be on one of the early anniversaries of 9/11. His team rallied around him and named him captain for the evening's game.

Andrew remembers feeling absolutely on fire that night as he made play after play—feeling more energized after each one. He says he felt his father there with him and that between the emotion of feeling Gary's presence and the support of all his teammates, he caught himself crying into his helmet more than once.

The parents of one of those teammates wrote down their experience of that evening and posted it on one of the memorial websites on the fifth anniversary of 9/11. Here's part of what they wrote:

Every person on Seton's team and every fan who made the journey to the game knew what today was and what young Andrew Bird had been going through emotionally all week. From the kickoff, Andrew and his teammates took control—a sack by Andrew, a fumble recovery, an interception. The parents cheering from the stands kept looking up at the sky, almost wondering if Gary himself was right there watching his beautiful son play the game of his life. Call it a presence, call it a Blessing or call it a proud dad watching his son from the best seat in the house. Seton won 56 to something, but the score didn't matter. After the game the players and coaches knelt down on the field next to the grandstands where all the fans were kneeling too. We all listened to the coach as he and Andrew's teammates dedicated the victory to Andrew and his outstanding performance. All the fans, parents, coaches and players prayed with tears streaming down our faces. Andrew spoke of his love for his father and of his gratitude for his mom, sister and teammates, and then he dedicated his and his team's performance to his father.

Andrew still talks to his father whenever he's going through a tough time and needs guidance and strength—even for something as simple as finishing a homework assignment or sorting out his finances. Andrew attends Arizona State University where he is working toward his degree in urban planning and sustainability. He can imagine one day owning his own firm dedicated to ensuring a clean and sustainable water supply for the people of Arizona.

He recently made the comment to someone that he doesn't know what the future holds for him in the way of family—only that he will always take care of his mother and sister because "that's what Dad would have done."

Amanda, too, remembers her dad as someone "who was always there," whether watching *The X-Files* over huge bowls of ice cream, sharing her excitement over getting the braces off her teeth, teaching her to ride a horse, or coming into her bedroom in the morning to kiss her goodbye before leaving for work. She will tell you that she knows her dad continues to watch over her because of the ease with which everything in her life falls into place. She is 25 now, with a bachelor's degree in conservation biology from ASU. She now lives in Newport Beach, California, where she works for an environmental non-profit organization focused on improving water quality and the health of marine habitats throughout the Southern California region. Her job is to work with local low-income high school students to help them increase their awareness of environmental issues through hands-on science experiments in natural settings. She also works part-time as a scuba instructor.

Amanda's list of goals includes enrolling in graduate school to pursue a career as a physical therapist. She currently takes classes in boxing and thinks she might someday like to compete in the sport, all while continuing to teach scuba lessons.

So much connects us all as a human family. Over the course of the past ten years, starting with the sound of Katie Couric's voice saying, *We have breaking news*, I have come to know with unwavering certainty that *nothing will separate us.*

I know because my connection, my relationship with Gary continued even though I could no longer hear his voice or hold his body close. In visions, dreams, acts of kindness performed in his name—even in a confirmation code for America West—the spirit that was the essence of him simply took another form.

I know *nothing will separate us* because in the time since 9/11, I've seen the proof played out among ever-widening circles of people around me. In the first few days, some people wrote to tell me that my loss inspired them to reach out to others who were grieving.

> *I watched you on television two weeks ago, the day before I drove to San Diego to be with friends who lost a son in the World Trade Center. Listening to you—someone I know and admire—changed all this from television to reality. I was inspired to get up the next morning and be with my friends— something I probably should have done a day or two earlier...*

Others wrote to say they were praying—not just for me, or even just for the victims of 9/11, but for the people of the world:

> *I am currently assisting "The Lost Boys" of the Sudan who have arrived here in Phoenix. There are six of these young men I'm especially close to. [They] have been in the United States only a few weeks, but have known the horrors of terrorism and war most of their lives. Last Tuesday, we all gathered together and watched the day's events unfold. That evening, we lit two candles in prayer, one for the innocent victims in Sudan, one for the people in the United States. Please know that you remain in the prayers of all seven of us. Our hearts are broken for each of you...*

As time went on, I began to receive letters from people who wanted me to know they were the recipients of gifts presented in Gary's name. One of these came from a teacher in nearby Mesa who worked in a program called "The Family Tree Project" in which low-income, non-English-speaking (primarily Hispanic) parents attend classes with their preschool-aged children. In Gary's memory, the Mesa Rotary Club had collected books for the children in this program to take home. The teacher shared newspaper accounts and photos of Gary and our family's experiences after 9/11. Despite the effort required, their parents insisted on writing to me in their fledgling

English to express their appreciation for the gift and for the reason behind it. One wrote that she had yet to lose a loved one, but she knew that day would come. She wanted me to know that when it did, she planned to do something to remember them and she hoped that her family would one day remember her by doing something good for someone else.

Another wrote simply:

We are so happy with the books and it is good to remember Gary. I talked to my son about him and I want him to feel so proud of Gary.

More than six years after the event, a woman from Mesa, Arizona, posted on one of the websites set up in honor of 9/11 victims:

As I read through all these wonderful letters I couldn't help but think of my six-month-old son, my husband and my family. To think of how fragile life is and what a beautiful human being Gary Bird must have been to his family. His face, smile and eyes look so caring. Although I don't know him or his family, somehow I found his name and picture. Maybe from heaven above this is a small part of him, a way of saying to his family: "Look. After all this time I am still here; I live in so many people's hearts, even those whom I do not know. I am still here and will not be forgotten"...

The most recent entry was posted on February 20 of this year. The message is unsigned.

I'm just someone from Scottsdale who never knew you, but wanted to say RIP and my heartfelt prayers to your family.

In the face of tragedy, the mind fills with questions: *How do I get through this? Am I strong enough? What am I supposed to do? How do I care for my children? What if I do the wrong thing? Does it matter? Can I ever again hold any hope for the future?*

I am here to tell you, from experience, there is no question the mind can ask that the love of God, of family, of friends and of our entire human community cannot answer. It is in that unbreakable connection that I found peace. It is there I found hope. It is there I found healing and joy.

It all begins with trusting the connection is there; surrendering yourself to the peace and care of God; watching for the signs God places in your path; and being willing to pick up the tools He provides to guide your way—whether in the form of people, books, songs, Scripture, dreams...

Signs and tools abound even in the most painful of circumstances. Look and you will find them.

It is not true that miracles only consist of saving people from the brink of death or bringing them back to life. For my children and me, the miracle was that, even though Gary's body was gone, love remained and peace resided in our hearts, our minds, our souls and in our house.

*The following words appear on a pedestal at the 9/11
Memorial in Phoenix, Arizona:*

Moving Memories

Memory is the sun that lights the material of history.

The sun moves.

The memory of September 11, 2001, casts a shadow from New York City,

Washington D.C., and Shanksville, Pennsylvania to, and through, us

here in Arizona.

It is the shadow of many decisions and nearly 3,000 lives lost.

This memorial intends to bring them to light for you.

Here, from ten in the morning until three in the afternoon,

the sun reveals descriptions of that day's decisions and reactions.

The sun moves.

Our memories appear then transform in time.

The combination of letters and shadows before you

represents the approximate number of people killed

in the attack.

That day's memory is made tangible by the piece of steel beam,

salvaged from the destroyed World Trade Center.

It rests on the concrete pedestal

that was mixed with rubble and dust from the Pentagon

and earth from Shanksville, Pennsylvania.

Decisions make history. Moving memories reveals it. The sun shines on us all.

Photo by Charlie Brown

Nothing Will Separate Us

The sun moves. Our memories appear and then transform in time.

Ten years have passed since thousands of people died in the World Trade Center, at the Pentagon and on a quiet field in Pennsylvania. To say they were killed by terrorist extremists does not say enough. They were killed by the merciless cruelty of hatred, prejudice and ignorance.

The view from Ground Zero today reflects a great deal of healing and work left to be done. Images posted on the World Trade Center website show the progress that has been made as well as the vision of what is to come.

The memorial will consist of two massive pools set in the footprints of the Twin Towers with the largest man-made waterfalls in the country cascading down the sides. The names of the nearly three-thousand individuals killed in the September 11 attacks and the February 1993 World Trade Center bombing will be inscribed around the edges.

Two of the original steel tridents from the Twin Towers will be enclosed in the Pavilion's grand glass atrium that guests will pass through to get to the entrance to the Memorial Museum.

Mine is among the families that have been invited to contribute remembrance materials of our lost loved ones. Among ours, Amanda, Andrew and I are sending the photograph of Gary that appears at the front of this book—head back, hand on his stomach, consumed with laughter. I've chosen that photo not only because it truly captures the spirit of who Gary was, but because it is important to me that the presence of joy, of love and of peace—not terrorism, not hatred, not destruction—be his legacy and the legacy of us all as a human family.

Fifty years ago the Pulitzer Prize for literature was awarded to an author whose book so brilliantly captures the human capacity for good, for evil, and for everything in between. I still have the copy of Harper Lee's *To Kill a Mockingbird* that Gary kept on our bookshelf. In it the mockingbird serves as the symbol of innocence in its purest form, as a creature that does no harm but exists solely to sing its heart out.

And that, Atticus Finch tells his children, is why it is a sin to kill a mockingbird.

My beloved companion was one of thousands of mockingbirds killed on 9/11— killed by people who didn't know them, never spoke with them, had no idea what lived inside their hearts.

My daughter and son lost their childhood innocence that day, as countless other daughters and sons have when seeing the face of evil for the first time.

How could they do it, how could they?

That is the question Atticus' daughter, Scout, asks when she learns a group of men shot and killed her father's client, Tom Robinson, a black man accused of rape but whose only crime was "to feel sorry for a white woman" at a time and a place where racial and social boundaries were firmly drawn and crossed by only the rarest of souls. Atticus represents that rare soul, the kind who, when his daughter asks whether it is okay to hate Hitler, answers: *It is not. It is not okay to hate anybody.*

Andrew was just thirteen years old when his father was killed. Thirteen. When Father Dale asked Andrew what he truly felt inside, this was his answer: *I'm happy for my dad, because I know he's in a better place. But I'm really mad at the people who did this.*

Today in the Arizona State Capitol Mall in Phoenix stands a memorial to 9/11. I was invited to serve as a member of the Governor's Commission appointed to oversee the private funding, design and construction of the project.

The memorial titled "Moving Memories" features time lines and a spectrum of emotional responses to 9/11 that have been laser cut into a circular steel canopy. As the sun moves overhead, these words appear in shadow on the concrete base below. The entire structure encircles a piece of steel salvaged from the World Trade Center

Photo by Charlie Brown

which rests on a pedestal made from concrete mixed with rubble from the Pentagon and soil from the field in Shanksville, Pennsylvania.

The first word on the timeline is "WHY." Beneath that are the words, "I'LL BE HOME FOR DINNER TUESDAY NIGHT"— Gary's parting words to me.

The sun moves. Our memories appear and then transform in time.

Photo by Charlie Brown

A fews days after the attack, before I knew whether or not Gary was still with us, news reporters presented me with the question of what I felt about the terrorists responsible. My answer then was the same as it is now: I wish for them all to be surrounded and transformed by the power of prayer. I wish for a better answer to give our children when they ask, *How could they do it?* than the only answer Atticus had to give:

I don't know, but they did it. They've done it before and they did it tonight and they'll do it again and when they do it—seems that only children weep.

Little more than a week into 2011, we Americans found ourselves reeling from the shooting deaths of six people in Tucson and the wounding of fourteen others, including Arizona congresswoman Gabrielle Giffords who was shot in the head. The assailant appeared to be a disturbed young man in his early twenties and his exact motives are as yet unknown.

Among the dead is a nine-year-old girl, Christina Taylor Green, once featured in the book *Faces of Hope* about children born on the day of the 9/11 terrorist attacks. Christina had just been elected to her student council and had come with a neighbor to meet Congresswoman Giffords because she wanted to learn more about public service. Her mother Roxanna Green was quoted as saying that her daughter often repeated the same sentiment:

"We are so blessed. We have the best life."

A New York firefighter brought the largest of the American flags that survived the collapse of the Twin Towers to Arizona to be at Christina's funeral.

Sadly, Atticus was right. They've done it before and they did it tonight and they'll do it again. Only this time—as we did after the Oklahoma City bombings, Columbine and too many other senseless acts of violence—we weep for a child.

The sun moves. Our memories appear and then transform in time.

In his closing statement to the jury, Atticus Finch points to the racial prejudice held by the prosecution's witnesses, prejudice he describes as based on an "evil assumption." How many evil assumptions, I wonder, lay at the root of all the grievances we hold against each other as human beings, from the pettiest to the most devastating? Atticus' son, Jem, destroys elderly Mrs. Dubose's flower garden as retribution for insults he believes are the products of a mean spirit. It isn't until she dies, leaving him a box containing a perfect bloom, that Jem learns her lashing out was the effect of withdrawing, by choice, from the morphine the doctor had prescribed for so long. Jem learns his father considers Mrs. Dubose to be "the bravest woman" he ever knew.

Who among us hasn't formed an opinion of another person, only to discover we misjudged them?

In Harper Lee's story, the "good" women of the Maycomb County missionary society get together to pray for the poor heathen souls of an African tribe that "had so little sense of family that the whole tribe was one big family." The women are appalled that the children had as many fathers and mothers as there were men and women in the community and thus believe their prayers are desperately needed to change the situation.

Throughout these years after 9/11, Amanda and Andrew have had as many fathers and mothers as are men and women in the community who have embraced us. People with children of their own sent money to help pay for my children's education. Other mothers took the time to look in on my children while they were at school. And I checked my e-mail one morning to find this message from my cousin Gloria in California:

Just to let you know, Bruce mentioned to me this morning that he would be honored to be Amanda's escort at any Father/Daughter dances that come up.

Brian can't wait to spend time with Andrew teaching him Adobe Premier and After Effects. Kevin can't wait to escort you to Colorado....

I thank God for this huge extended family of ours. Which raises another question about our human condition. What if even in our most fervent prayers—like the women of the Maycomb County missionary society—we are praying for the wrong things? Things that do more to divide us than to bring us together? What might be possible if all our prayers were aligned?

I remembered something Jem had once explained to me when he went
through a brief period of psychical research: he said if enough people—
a stadium full, maybe—were to concentrate on one thing, such as setting
a tree afire in the woods, that the tree would ignite of its own accord.
I toyed with the idea of asking everyone below to concentrate on setting
Tom Robinson free, but thought if they were as tired as I, it wouldn't work.

I don't wish to allow anything or anyone—not even the men who took the love of my life from me—to make me tired and cynical. No matter how my children and I may weep over our loss, I refuse to waste my energy on anger and hatred. I want to be counted among the stadium filled with people, all concentrating on igniting a fire. I wish to live by the words of the Prayer of St. Francis: *Where there is hatred, let me sow love.*

That is what Gary would want. He stood for the safety and well-being of the innocent, whether they be children, animals or grown men working in the mines.

The sun moves. Our memories appear and then transform in time.

In the months leading up to the tenth anniversary of 9/11 we have witnessed historic events—here in Arizona and on the international stage—that continue to confront each of us with the question of how we choose to respond. In March, the Arizona legislature passed a bill calling for the removal of certain panels from the 9/11 memorial outside the capital building—panels containing eleven phrases that some lawmakers considered objectionable. In leading the fight to revise the memorial—a memorial designed through a process of public hearings and paid for by private funds—one Arizona legislator characterized these eleven phrases as "political," "controversial" and even "offensive."

He later withdrew his objection to the reference to the death of Balbir Singh Sodhi. Sodhi, a Sikh, was shot and killed four days after 9/11 by a man who presumed he must have been an Arab simply because he wore a turban. According to the *Arizona Republic*, this legislator later apologized to Sodhi's family, admitting he had not understood that his killing was a hate crime prompted by the 9/11 terrorist attacks.

However, he stood by his opposition to ten other phrases that appear on the memorial. These include:

• Fear of foreigners

• Foreign born Americans afraid

• Feeling of invincibility lost

- Must bomb back
- You don't win battles of terrorism with more battles
- Violent acts leading US to war: 05 07 1915, 12 07 1941, 08 04 1964 & 09 11 2001
- 06 03 02 Congress questions why CIA & FBI didn't prevent attacks
- FBI agent issues July 2001 warning in "Phoenix Memo"
- 03 13 02 New Afghan leader elected
- Middle East violence motivates attacks in U.S.

The Arizona legislator publicly characterized the phrases as "disrespectful to the memories of those who died on 9/11." As the wife of one who died on that day, a wife with boundless and unceasing respect for her husband's memory, I felt compelled to write a letter to Arizona Governor Jan Brewer, appealing to her to veto the bill that would dismantle our state's 9/11 memorial. I felt it my responsibility to speak—not only on my own behalf, but for Gary. I wrote that if Gary were here, if it were someone other than he who was killed that day, he would honor the wishes and sentiments expressed by the loved ones of those lost. Having lived his life as one of great and constant personal integrity, I also know he would insist upon the integrity of a public display such as the memorial and not to alter events, or edit out the facts, simply to promote a political agenda.

I added that Gary would have seen this move to dismantle and rewrite the 9/11 memorial nearly ten years after the event as the antithesis of healing, of moving on. It takes energy from building community and diverts it to reigniting debate and discord over what it means to be "pro-American."

I closed my appeal to Governor Brewer with the question that if a memorial treasured by so many could be taken apart because of words one man finds "offensive," what would keep someone else from attempting to remove Gary's last words to me for no other reason than they deemed such a personal statement inappropriate for a public memorial?

I am grateful to Governor Brewer for choosing to veto the bill. In her veto letter concerning the memorial, she wrote, "In recent days, I have heard concerns from some of the Arizona families directly affected by the 9/11 attacks and their aftermath. For their sake, I am sorry this issue has reared its head once more."

My hope is that Governor Brewer's action puts an end to the bickering and lays the matter of the memorial to rest once and for all. I believe God has invited us all to choose greater callings.

The sun moves. Our memories appear and then transform in time.

Since the tragic events of 9/11, Gary has moved on. The children and I have moved on. We, as a nation, have done our very best to move on. Fighting with each other only serves to polarize and set us back. It chips away at the spirit of community that brought us all together as Americans and as global citizens, united in our refusal to let terrorism tear us apart.

The death of Osama bin Laden invites a myriad of possible responses—politically, emotionally and spiritually. Like millions of people around the world, I watched the events unfold on my television. At ten o'clock that evening, a young reporter stood at my front door, asking me what I was feeling. She looked uncomfortable, even apologetic, as though she wished her editor had chosen somebody—*anybody*—other than her for this assignment. She almost looked relieved when I politely told her that I was choosing not to give any interviews on the subject. She apologized for disturbing me and left.

Later that night, with the help of my neighbor Deb, the publicist, I sent out a brief statement to the media on behalf of my children and me. I expressed our support and gratitude for our leaders and our armed forces, as well as for the ongoing spirit of community that continues not only to sustain me and my children, but also unites us as a human family.

I could choose to stand and cheer in front of the media and anyone who cares to listen over the death of this man who masterminded the attacks that took Gary from our family. No one I know would find fault if I did. The truth is, I feel no desire to celebrate Osama bin Laden's death. I disavowed any attachment to his fate nearly ten years ago when I surrendered my own into the hands of God. I choose instead to pray for his soul and for the souls of those still living who might seek to commit hate-fueled acts of violence.

In my friend Donna's dream, Gary wanted everyone to know the true story of 9/11. I, like so many people around the world, have searched for whatever grains of truth are to be found in the ashes. And the truths I have found over these past ten years are these:

The power to prevail over pain and loss lies in letting go of fear and anger and surrendering all things to God (by whatever name He is known).

The invitation to surrender is ever present.

In that sacred moment of surrender, the mind, heart and soul open to receive God's healing miracles.

The miracles appear through our unending, unbreakable connection to God and each other.

Nothing—neither death nor life, neither past nor future, nor anything in creation—will be able to separate us from the love of God.

Nothing outside the love of God—neither death nor life, neither past nor future, nor anything in creation—possesses the power to separate us as God's children. We hold the power to be, for each other and our world, instruments of peace.

If there is meaning in the first two letters in the airline confirmation code my cousin received for the trip to Gary's memorial—TRBIRD—I may never know what it is. But the initials for *Tom Robinson* seem fitting enough. Both he and Gary were mockingbirds. Both were kind, loving people who should not have died because of hatred and ignorance.

Both are examples of the best in human nature, of the love, peace and goodness that are within our power to create. In our families. In our work. In our communities. In our world. Every day.

Every time.

(These are the wishes expressed by Melissa Woodward,
my niece, when she was in second grade.)

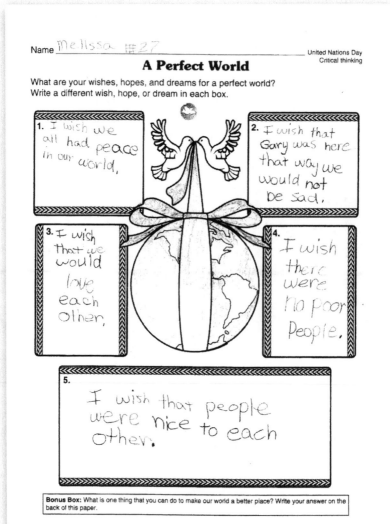

97

Home Movies

The videotape of our last summer together as family recently turned up in the bottom drawer of a living room cabinet. Every scene is dated in the bottom right hand corner.

Here's Gary on June 17, riding on the seat of his John Deere tractor mower as it cuts the grass growing in the pasture. He steers in the direction of where I'm standing along the fence line. He waves and tips his baseball cap. As soon as he is close enough to make himself heard over the engine noise, he opens his mouth and sings: *She thinks my tractor's sexy...*

The purpose of the video is to record for Amanda and Andrew the christening of their Father's Day gift: a John Deere tractor mower umbrella to shade their dad from the blistering Arizona summer sun.

As he rides past the camera on his mower, I remark to him how much he looks like Forrest Gump. I then turn my attention to Lil and Caty Lu in the corral. I mention that Bobbi has been gone about four days, having started her summer study program in Italy. I want to record for her just how much Caty Lu has grown in that time.

Amanda's summer dance recital comes next, followed by the first moments of our family vacation to Disneyland.

It opens with Gary at our hotel, walking down the hall toward our room where I'm filming from the doorway.

"Here comes Goofy," he says in his best Goofy cartoon character impression. "That's how you know you're at Disneyland!"

Over the next several days, we all take turns behind the camera, recording highlights of our trip. Here we are on the Jungle Ride and coming off the Matterhorn. Here we are on Big Thunder Mountain's runaway train as the scenery rushes by in a blur.

And here we are on the Disneyland Railroad, Gary sandwiched between Amanda and me as we rest our heads on his shoulders.

Our last video of Gary was taken on September 2, 2001. It is short—just a few minutes of Gary and his friend Jonathan giving Amanda and her best friend Kristi a scuba diving lesson in our backyard swimming pool. While the girls practice using the equipment, Jonathan stands waist-deep in the shallow end, giving directions loud enough for them to hear underwater. Meanwhile Gary floats on the surface, breathing through a snorkel and watching every move they make.

It is a portrait of a loving family man, adventurous spirit and passionate risk manager in action—no more and no less an accurate reflection of Gary as any other moment in his life.

That alone probably says everything there is to know about him.

Family Album

This was taken around Christmas of 2000 (there's that artificial tree again). We were about to leave for a fundraising event for the Tempe Boys and Girls Club. We both looked forward to these kinds of events. For one thing, we both loved the feeling that came with supporting anything that supports the welfare of children. For another, we enjoyed getting together with all the friends we had made over the years through Gary's work with the organization. Plus, it was another excuse to go dancing.

I liked to sing to Gary out on the dance floor. For our first wedding dance, Gary chose the song co-written and performed by Barbara Streisand: *Evergreen.* Our wedding video captures me softly singing the words into Gary's ear.

The last time I sang to Gary was at the annual Tempe Governor's Ball. He led me to the dance floor and as the band played, I sang the words:

Have I told you lately that I love you?

Gary and I told each other "I love you" on the last morning we spent together, just before Gary left to catch his flight to New York. More importantly we lived those words every day of our marriage. Because we did, I was able to release him without a single regret.

I agree with Andrew when he says how important it is to live each day to the fullest, and with Amanda when she advises never to pass up an opportunity to give someone you love a big, long hug. They learned those lessons from their father.

Thank you, Gary.

I love you.

Andrew, Donna and Amanda

Acknowledgments

There are so many people to whom I owe deep personal thanks for assistance with this book. The love and support we have received over the past decade have come from a vast network of family, friends, neighbors, fellow parishioners, colleagues, public figures and compassionate strangers. These comprise the various "communities" that have risen up around me, wrapped me in their hugs and carried us forward together. I know in my heart that my children and I have been the focus of prayers whispered by people we may never meet. I am forever grateful to each and every one of you. I wish you peace...the peace that surpasses all understanding.

Donna M. Killoughey Bird
August 2011

Romans 8: 28-39

28 And we know that in all things God works for the good of those who love Him, who have been called according to His purpose.

29 For those God foreknew he also predestined to be conformed to the likeness of his Son, that he might be the firstborn among many brothers.

30 And those he predestined, he also called; those he called, he also justified; those he justified, he also glorified.

31 What, then, shall we say in response to this? If God is for us, who can be against us?

32 He who did not spare his own Son, but gave him up for us all—how will he not also, along with him, graciously give us all things?

33 Who will bring any charge against those whom God has chosen? It is God who justifies.

34 Who is he that condemns? Jesus Christ who died—more than that, who was raised to life—is at the right hand of God and is also interceding for us.

35 Who shall separate us from the love of Christ? Shall trouble or hardship or persecution or famine or nakedness or danger or sword?

36 As it is written: "For your sake we face death all day long; we are considered as sheep to be slaughtered."

37 No, in all these things we are more than conquerors through him who loved us.

38 For I am convinced that neither death nor life, neither angels nor demons, neither the present nor the future, nor any powers,

39 neither height nor depth, nor anything else in all creation, will be able to separate us from the love of God that is in Christ Jesus our Lord.

New International Version, Archaeological Study Bible
© 2005 by the Zondervan Corp.